Creation

On the Origin of Man

An RS teacher's investigation of the Bible, scientific evidence and diversity of thought

Karsten Wille

Copyright © 2020 Karsten Wille

All rights reserved. No part of this publication may be reproduced, distributed, or transmitted in any form or by any means, including photocopying, recording, or any other electronic or mechanical methods, without the prior written permission of the publisher, except in the case of brief quotations embodied in critical reviews and certain other noncommercial uses permitted by copyright law. For permission, write to the publisher at the address below:

Greatness University Publishers
info@greatness-university.com
www.greatnessuniversity.co.uk

ISBN: 978-1-913164-57-7
ISBN-13: 978-1-913164-57-7

DEDICATION

I would like to dedicate this book to my Father.

CONTENTS

Acknowledgments	i
Preface	1
Is Science Atheistic?	3
The Catholic Perception	7
The Evangelical Perception	17
The Bible and Scientific Discovery	33
Evolution and the Origins of life	49
Small Successive Mutations	59
Missing Links	67
The Fruits of Darwinism	81
Summary	93
Bibliography	131

ACKNOWLEDGMENTS

I would like to thank my friends and family and particularly Pastor Rob Payne for the many hours we have spent together discussing this very subject. A special thanks to my mother for helping me with the editing.

PREFACE

There has never been a published scientific work that has shaped the world into a streamlined view, permeating the way we perceive the physical, biological and psychological sciences today such as Darwin's book 'On the Origins of Species'. His work has not just been confined to these fields, but has influenced both history and Christian Theology as well. The findings of Darwin have been readily accepted as a suitable explanation for the beginning of all life by the Catholic Church and other liturgical denominations.

This book seeks to question the validity of Darwin's 'On the Origins of Species', and whether it should be accepted by the Church as a suitable alternative to scripture. This will include the difficult task of discussing philosophy and science as a whole. The non-literalist interpretation of scripture will require separating truth in two perceived forms.

Scientific truth: Facts that can be proven scientifically.

Theological truth: Things we believe which require faith.

To the contrary, the literalist believer of God's word (Evangelicals) will view science and theology as synonymous, very much in line with St Augustine. There seems to be a growing trend in recent history that views science as the privileged practice of the Atheist. Historically though, some scientists associated closely to their denominations and held the Bible in high regard, whereas for others the Bible stood out as their very foundation for a life and belief system.

If we look scripturally at the very origins of human life, it is difficult to ignore what the Bible tells us in Genesis, that Adam was formed from the dust of the earth, and that God breathed into Adam's nostrils and he became a living soul. Evolution teaches that humanity was formed from the primordial soup. This is something we will be looking at in greater detail as we dissect what Darwin actually said in his work, including the pitfalls Darwin sets as the limitations of his hypothesis. Could it be that Darwin needs to be re-interpreted in view of the science we have available to us today?

I will approach this by exploring Darwin's theory and what leading evolutionists say regarding their own system of belief according to the evidence that is available. We will also evaluate if the Bible has any scientific significance in the exploration of our origins. Lastly, we will explore history and the impact Darwinian survival of the fittest has had on society as a whole.

IS SCIENCE ATHEISTIC?

I would first like to address a very important issue, especially in the current climate of relative recent history. There seems to be a lot of credence in the world attributed to those who have a complete atheistic philosophy of science. Even if the word 'intelligent design', appears in any scientific paper, many universities clamp down on it heavily as if some unspoken moral law of science has been broken. This is very surprising, especially if we historically look at the people who contributed to science.

One only needs to make an encyclopedia search in regard to Christians who contributed to science and technology and vast numbers of names are thrown into the forefront. These were people who identified themselves as Christians in their public life or at least adhered strictly to the denomination they were part of. If we consider some of the people and their accomplishments before the 18th century we notably have an exhaustive list of scientists of which I can only mention a few. The Bishop of Lincoln Robert Grosseteste (1175 - 1253), is highly regarded as the founder of scientific thought in Oxford. He did much for evidence-based science, writing papers on optics, astronomy and geometry. The Patron saint of scientists in Catholicism was Albertus Magnus (1193-1280), who expressed the need to study causation. Jean Buridan (1300-1358) was both a philosopher and priest. He developed the theory of Impetus, which explains objects in freefall. This was the forerunner for the studies of Galileo and Sir Isaac Newton's principles of inertia. Nicole Oresme (1323-1382) was a theologian and bishop of Lisieux. He had many contributions to science, including the discovery of refraction and curvature of light. Nicholas of Cusa (1401- 1464) who was a Catholic Cardinal and theologian, was one of the forerunners to heliocentrism, moving away from the popular geocentric view of the time. Otto Brunfels (1488-1534) was an outspoken theologian and botanist. He is well known as literally the father of botany. Ignazie Dani (1536-1586), Bishop of Alatari was a mathematician and astronomer and contributed to science in revolutionary engineering. Francis Bacon (1561 – 1626) pioneered experimental science, very much in the same vein as scientific methods today. As mentioned earlier, Galileo (1564 – 1642) was an astronomer, physicist, engineer, philosopher and mathematician who was outstanding in all these fields. Blaise Pascal (1623 – 1662) had much to contribute in Physics (Pascal's law), Maths (Pascal's theorem) and theology (Pascal's Wager). Robert Boyle (1627 – 1691) argued that science was also the study of the glory of God. His work is well known in the field of Chemistry. Sir Isaac Newton (1643 – 1727) completed studies of objects in freefall during the scientific revolution and is a physicist who discovered the laws of gravity.

Coming up to the 18th century, the contributions to science continue with John Ray (1627- 1705), a botanist, who was the first person to define the concept of species. Gottfried Leibniz (1646 – 1716) was a philosopher who developed the theory of pre-established harmony, putting forward the design argument. He also contributed to mathematics, physics, technology and geology. Antonie van Leuwenhoek (1632 – 1723) is known today as the father of microbiology. Emanuel Swedenborg (1688 – 1772) hypothesized the origins of the solar system. Albrecht von Haller (1708 – 1777) was an anatomist and physiologist renowned as the father of modern physiology. Antoine Lavoisier (1743 – 1794) was known as the father of chemistry. Carl Linnaeus (1707 – 1778) a botanist, physician and zoologist, was credited as the father of modern-day taxonomy.

Moving onto the 19th century, Joseph Priestly (1733- 1804) was credited with the discovery of oxygen. The first battery was discovered by Alessandro Volta (1745 - 1827). This is how we get the word Volt. William Kirby (1759 - 1850) is best known for chemistry and introducing the atomic theory. Goerges Cuvier (1769 - 1832) was known as the father of paleontology. Andre Marie Ampere (1775 - 1836), was one of the founders of electromagnetism. Amps are named after him. John Abercrombie (1780 - 1844) developed theories on neuropathology. John Steven Henslow (1796- 1861) was a priest, botanist and geologist who secured a place on HMS Beagle for Charles Darwin. Bernhard Riemann (1826 - 1866) contributed to mathematics and general relativity. William Whewell (1794 - 1866) was credited with many scientific words we use today such as 'scientist', 'physicist', 'anode' and 'cathode'. Michael Faraday (1791 - 1867) contributed to electromagnetic theory and electrolysis in chemistry. Gregor Mendel (1822 - 1884) was an Augustine Abbot, who did much research on pea plants in the monetary garden in Austria and is known as the father of modern genetics. He discovered no genetic changes in species over generations, introducing the 'laws of constant elements', (constant species) determining an organism's traits. This was at odds with Darwin's suggestion of plant evolution over time. Heinrich Hertz (1857 - 1894) was a physicist who was able to evidence the existence of electromagnetic waves. Joseph Lister (1827 - 1912) was a surgeon and known for ground breaking studies in antiseptic surgery.

The 20th century notably recorded 65.5% of Nobel Prize winners as people with strong links to Christianity. George Lemaitre (1894 - 1966) was a Jesuit priest from Belgium and was the first person to propose and develop the Big Bang theory. George Lemaitre's proposal gained much enthusiasm from Einstein.

These are just some legendary scientists we know, who were not just outstanding in their field, but also many were well regarded theologians. Some associated closely to their denominations and held the Bible in high regard, whereas, for others the Bible stood out as their very foundation for life and belief system. The important point we can glean from this; is that *Science* and *Religion* was not an issue. The workings of their faith did not inhibit their ability to contribute to science: it was actually very much a part of it. The strange concept of defining scientists exclusively as people who interpret the world through a lens of atheism cannot therefore be substantiated by history.

THE CATHOLIC PERCEPTION

It is difficult to speak on this subject without first acknowledging the amount of work that has gone into the perception created by the use of art in the Catholic Church. Michelangelo's 'Creation of Adam' painting is the first image most people have in their minds when considering the origins of humanity. The beautiful thing about art is that it can convey and express ideas that words cannot fully explain. Over the centuries people visited Cathedrals and had access to the word of God simply by the communication of the art work on the walls, whether stain glass windows, mosaics or frescos. The Sistine Chapel holds the most famous example of art, seeking to describe scenes from the book of Genesis.

This piece of art reflects many teachings of the Catholic Church, in that Adam is shown as a perfect man of strength and painted as an image of the goodness of God (Genesis 1:31). He is stretching out his hand to God in an attempt to become fully alive, communicating the omnipotence of his creator. It is the very dependency on God that is conveyed by this earthen vessel. God is seen as the ancient of days, full of glory and splendour, reinforced by the notion that Adam is created, not just in God's image, but also his likeness. The concept of the desire of relationship between God and man is apparent, with clear hints of mutual appreciation. We see the transcendence of God in the manner of his sweeping through the air, equally the limitations of the human man, who is firmly grounded on an immovable foundation. The painting re-enforces the omnipotence of God, reminding us that nothing exists that was not first made by him.

Genesis 1 in scripture communicates the nature of God. The Catholic Church views this, however, as a myth that describes the creation of all things, with the emphasis on the omnipotence of God. This omnipotence is shown as he forms the world with the power of speech, and everything he says comes into being following his word. He is beyond earth, space (transcendent) and time and requires nothing else than his verbal release to bring everything into being. The concept of creating something from nothing (ex nihilo) is the main question this book seeks to address. He is the only person who can do it. He created the world perfect and everything he created as stated in Genesis 1 was good.

The teaching of the Church, however, does not translate into a scientific account of creation. The Church carefully distinguishes between two types of perceived truths. One truth to be seen as theological truth, and the other as scientific truth.

These ideas are defined as follows:

Scientific truth: Facts that can be proven scientifically.

Theological truth: Things we believe which require faith.

This encourages the philosophy, that in Genesis 1, the relationship with God, the environment and with humanity is explained. The Catholic Church does not believe in the literal six days of creation, with God resting on the seventh. This belief does however enforce the idea that God created the universe and world over larger periods of time, which does not negate the love he has for humanity. Therefore, the church does not believe the account in Genesis 1 to be considered historical. As humans were created on the last day in this perceived myth, we are considered to be the most important of his creation, as described in Genesis 1:27:

'God created humankind in his image'. **Genesis 1:27**

This idea also suggests we share qualities with God, not shared with the animal kingdom, in that we can give love, empathy and are capable of immense knowledge.

The Catholic Church does not view Genesis 1 and Genesis 2 as synonymous. It is actually believed that Genesis 2 is likely to have been written before Genesis 1. In other words, two separate creation stories. Genesis 2 holds the importance of the value of humanity, when God breathes life into Adam by his breath (Hebrew: Ru'ach), and Adam becomes a living soul. This indicates that we share the breath or even Spirit of God. Humanity is provided for in the Garden of Eden, and the planting of the tree in the middle of their paradise paves a way for free will, so humans are not created as robots. God gives them the choice to eat from the tree of the knowledge of good and evil, and does not actively prevent them from taking from its fruit as he also provides the element of free will. The account can easily be translated into God either providing for them, or through choice, man through their own decision providing for themselves.

God presents the animals to Adam to be named one by one, indicating that humanity has been given both authority and responsibility over them. When he names them, and it is discovered there is none suitable as a helper for him, God causes Adam to fall into a deep sleep and creates Eve from Adam's rib. This is a picture of the first marriage, in that two are both divided, but one.

The significance of this account also reflects God's transcendence. The beauty and complexity of creation with the vastness of the universe again shows his omnipotence, with the crown of his creation, humanity, made in his image and likeness; therefore, sharing the distinct nature of God. Humanity is able to have a relationship with God, because of the traits we share. This however, does bring with it responsibility as stewards of creation, to care for God's entire work. As God is the creator of all things, Catholics feel they have to respect creation, to ensure that nothing in creation is destroyed or undervalued. As God made everything perfect, everything he created is, therefore, an expression of himself. Human duty is thus to manage the world, and protect everything which is contained in it. The philosophy of stewardship is implied in Genesis 1:28:

[28] Then God blessed them, and God said to them, "Be fruitful and multiply; fill the earth and subdue it; have dominion over the fish of the sea, over the birds of the air, and over every living thing that [a] moves on the earth'. **Genesis 1:28**

Catholics believe that it is the responsibility of all generations to look after what they have inherited, and to pass on creation in a better state than it has been left. In other words, as unspoiled as possible!

The importance of humanity being created in God's Image and likeness, is reflected in the need to consider the dignity of all human beings. This translates into the principle of everyone being of equal value as we are all loved into existence by God. Humans are not just important to God, but also to one another. Sexual union is a way of a man and woman to express their humanity. Marriage is thus a sacrament in the Catholic Church. Free will was a gift from God to humanity, so people may express it freely. However, this gift also comes with responsibility to respect not just the dignity of others, but also yourself, as everyone has been made a child of God. Catholics also respect the idea of the sanctity of life as one of the main factors of the significance of the creation account. This is the belief, that all life is holy, precious and a gift from God. Therefore, every stage of life from embryonic form to the last breath is to be treated with dignity.

It is the eternal theological truth found in scripture which is important to Catholics, not the interpretation of literal truths in the form of a historical account of creation. The creation accounts are viewed as appealing to different audiences in a time that had different cultures, or cultural understandings of the events. It is the general belief that the creation stories in Genesis 2 were written down and recorded in 950 BC, whereas Genesis 1 was written later in 450 BC. These are treated as two separate creation accounts; however, the core value remains the same and doesn't contradict itself. The core values can be communicated as the following:

- Humanity is the Steward of Creation
- We are all created in the Image and Likeness of God
- There is nothing in creation that was not originally made by God.

- Everything that God created was good.

Catholic writings make the following point:

'Since God speaks in Sacred Scripture through men in human fashion; the interpreter of sacred scripture.... should carefully investigate what meaning the sacred writers really intended, and what God wanted to manifest by means of their words. To search out the intention of the sacred writers, attention should be given, among other things, to 'literary forms'. **Dei Verbum 12**

It isn't difficult to conjecture from the above synopsis that the Catholic Church leans to scientific truth over the non-literal interpretations of the Genesis accounts. Pope Francis made the following statement to cement any confusion of the teaching of the Church regarding this phenomenon:

'When we read in Genesis the account of Creation, we risk imagining God as a magician, with a magic wand able to make everything. But that is not so.....creation continued for.....millennia and millennia, until it became what we know today, precisely because God is not a ......conjurer, but the Creator who gives birth to all things. The beginning of the world is not the work of chaos,....but derives directly from a supreme Origin who creates out of love. The **Big Bang***.....does not contradict the divine act of creating, but rather requires it. The evolution of nature does not contrast with the notion of Creation, as evolution presupposes the creation of beings that evolve'.* **Pope Francis, 27 October 2014**

The Catholic Church is very proud of achievements in science. The contribution made by the physical sciences to examining these questions is stressed by the *Catechism*, which states:

> *"The question about the origins of the world and of man has been the object of many scientific studies which have splendidly enriched our knowledge of the age and dimensions of the cosmos, the development of life-forms and the appearance of man. These discoveries invite us to even greater admiration for the greatness of the Creator, prompting us to give him thanks for all his works and for the understanding and wisdom he gives to scholars and researchers"* **(CCC 283).**

I have spent the first chapter of this book outlining contributions by Christians to science, however the Catholic Church specifically celebrates the following people.

1. St Albert the Great, was a lecturer in theology and made many contributions in a variety of scientific fields. He was made the patron Saint of scientists.
2. Jean Baptiste Lamarck, is credited with pioneering an early form of **evolution** labelled Lamarckism.
3. Gregor Mendel, pioneered genetics; especially famous were his studies of pea plants in the monastery garden in Austria.
4. George Lemaitre, a Jesuit priest and scientist, was the first person to propose the **Big Bang** theory, which is the predominant scientific thought regarding the beginning of the universe till this day.

The Big Bang and the theory of evolution are not seen as compatible with scripture. However, if we take the example of George Lemaitre; he treated his scientific theories and his personal walk with God as something very different. In the 1950 encyclical *Humani generis*, Pope Pius XII confirmed that there is no intrinsic conflict between Christianity and the theory of evolution, provided that Christians believe that God created all things and that the individual soul is a direct creation by God and not the product of purely material forces. Creationists suggest the world was ordered and structured in a period of 6 days according to Genesis 1, whereas evolutionists would suggest, that the order is mostly the same, but the expanses of time are different. What if you stretched the time of Genesis from seven 'days' to seven 'ages' (lengths of time)? After all the Hebrew word for 'day' (Yom) can be interpreted as 'age' in certain circumstances. This could mean the world was formed over a longer (seven ages) period of time, instead of 7 days in Genesis 1.

The Magisterium encouraged the importance of both science and religion to be compatible; therefore, mutually supportive following the second Vatican council. Catholic scientists are encouraged to use their expertise to assist people grasp the nature and purpose of God's creation. Religion and Science may indeed see issues under a different lens, not through contradiction, but rather due to the diversity of questioning. A main point to be made within Catholicism is that scientific evidence explains the 'how', whereas, religion explores and confirms the 'why', dividing the two truths described earlier as 'scientific truth', and 'theological truth'.

Vatican 2 specifically has the following attitude to science in Gaudium et Spes:

'If methodical investigation within every branch of learning is carried out in a genuinely scientific manner and in accord with moral forms, it never truly conflicts with faith, for earthly matters and the concerns of faith derive from the same God'.
Gaudium et Spes 36

The Catholic Church in the interpretation of the Genesis accounts, puts caring for the environment as one of the most important principles. This is translated into a New Covenant principle by the following verses and commandments in Mark:

'The first is, 'Hear, O Israel: The Lord our God, the Lord is one; you shall love the Lord your God with all year heart, and with all your soul, and with all your mind, and with all your strength.' The second is this, 'You shall love your neighbour as yourself'. There is no other commandment greater than these'. **Mark 12:29-31**

This again places the emphasis on looking after the environment for many generations to come. Environmental politics plays a big part, especially in more recent Catholic thought and forms the crux of Catholic belief in regard to the relevance of Genesis, not historical accuracy or a literal scientific account of the origin of humanity.

Creation: On the Origin of Man

THE EVANGELICAL PERCEPTION

Literalist interpretation of scripture or specifically the book of Genesis could not be more different. Non-literalist reflection of Genesis possibly alludes more to the existence of merely a supreme higher force, rather than the carefully documented evidence brought to us in the Bible. Viewing the 'Creation of Adam' painting by Michelangelo in the Sistine Chapel also represents this notion. In the painting, Adam is brought to life by the touch of God, rather than the forming of the first man from the dust of the earth and God breathing into him life; therefore, becoming a living soul:

⁷And the LORD *God formed man of the dust of the ground, and breathed into his nostrils the breath of life; and man became a living soul'.* **Genesis 2:7**

Semantics, therefore, when reviewing scripture in the context it was written, thus becomes very important to the literalist. In this chapter we will view this importance of the Evangelical perception of the origins of man.

When we think of "science," we usually think of the study of the natural world; that which can be quantitatively measured—subjects such as biology and physics. Historically though, of the "natural" sciences, only geometry and astronomy were part of the standard university curriculum. So, what was a science? Evangelicals do not separate the concept of having one truth for one thing and another truth for another. Science and theological truth are therefore one and the same thing. I cannot divide your truth, my truth and their truth. There is just one truth, anything else is likely to be just someone else's opinion with all the biases that go along with it. Augustine defined science as: 'anything to do with knowledge of the temporal world'. Thomas Aquinas considered theology a science because it encounters 'special and general revelation'. It is worth noting, that Augustine was more in line with the literal interpretation of the Genesis accounts. Concerning creation, he writes:

'Perhaps we ought not to think of these creatures at the moment they were produced as subject to the processes of nature which we now observe in them, but rather as under the wonderful and unutterable power of the Wisdom of God, which reaches from end to end mightily and governs all graciously. For this power of Divine Wisdom does not reach by stages or arrive by steps. It was just as easy, then, for God to create everything as it is for Wisdom to exercise this mighty power. For through Wisdom all things were made, and the motion we now see in creatures, measured by the lapse of time, as each one fulfils its proper function, comes to creatures from those causal reasons implanted in them, which God scattered as seeds at the moment of creation when **He spoke and they were made, He commanded and they were created.** *Creation, therefore, did not take place slowly in order that a slow development might be implanted in those things that are slow by nature; nor were the ages established at plodding pace at which they now pass. Time brings about the development of these creatures according to the laws of their numbers, but there was no passage of time when they received these laws at creation'.*

Augustine. *The Literal Meaning of Genesis,* translated by John Hammond Taylor (1982), Vol. 1, Book 4, Chapter 33, paragraph 51-52, p. 141, italics in the original. New York: Newman Press.

Creation: On the Origin of Man

(St. Augustine of Hippo: Photo credit Wikipedia)

The Bible and a theological standard thus become of utmost importance. Although the scholastic standard has changed in our world, a Christian's belief in biblical inerrancy supports theology as "queen." It is not in the remit of a Bible believing Christian to pick and choose which parts of scripture to include and others to ignore. The Bible warns us to avoid "the opposing ideas of what is falsely called knowledge" (1 Timothy 6:20). Rather, we should strive to "correctly handle the word of truth" (2 Timothy 2:15). Putting scripture in context is of utmost importance. Theology truly is the starting place for learning. "The fear of the LORD is the beginning of knowledge" (Proverbs 1:7).

Evangelicals consider Genesis as a true historical and scientific account of the very origin of man, but why? From a literary sense, it therefore becomes important to distinguish between the genres the Bible is written in. When comparing genres of the Bible, one has: historical, poetry, wisdom, prophecy, Gospels (biography & parables) and finally epistles. The grammatical forms of the Hebrew thus become very important as they indicate what genre of writing is taking place. Hebrew uses special grammatical forms for the recording of history, which is the precise forms used in Genesis 1 to 11. This grammatical structure of historical narrative is continued from chapter 12 onwards, into Exodus, Joshua and Judges, which no one suggests is taken as allegory or poetry. The recording of history is the same throughout in those precise grammatical forms. (Steven W. Boyd)

The analysis of language is crucial, especially taking close note of who is speaking. If we take Jesus for example, would he really be speaking about a mythical couple when referring to Adam and Eve as a real historical narrative?

*⁴And He answered and said to them, "**Have you not read** that He who [a]made them at the beginning 'made them **male** and **female**,'⁵ and said, 'For this reason a **man** shall leave his father and mother and be joined to his wife, and the two shall become one flesh'?* **Matthew 19: 4-5**

*⁶But from the beginning of the creation, God 'made them male and female.'⁷ 'For this reason a **man** shall leave his father and mother and be joined to his wife, ⁸and the two shall become one flesh'; so then they are no longer two, but one* *flesh. ⁹ Therefore what God has joined together, let not man separate."* **Mark 10: 6-9**

It is important to realize when reading the above verses that Jesus is not telling a parable, neither is he speaking in allegory or prose. He is recalling an actual factual event which has taken place. The clear reference to Adam as a man does not open up the possibility of referring to a being who has not yet reached that status in the appearance of an ape-like ancestor. There are scores of verses confirming the historical events of Genesis, including Abel, Noah and Lot in the Gospels alone.

The ancestral line of course throws up more possibilities for scriptural discussion. Family trees provide interesting reading, whereby people recently have been fascinated researching their own records on ancestry websites, even as far as giving DNA samples to be sent away for analysis. There is nowhere in history, a better and more accurate recording system than that of the Jewish scribes. You may wonder why this is important? The genealogy in Matthew 1 follows the line of Joseph, though traditionally, Luke 3 outlines the lineage of Mary, the mother of Jesus all the way back to Adam. The family tree is thus complete, name by name from Adam to Jesus. The Gospel of Luke is also the Gospel outlining Jesus as the perfect Saviour. To suggest these records are fabricated is denying their historical value. The question would then have to be asked again: Which parts of scripture would you agree are factual or entering the realm of mythology? This carefully documents genealogy, of which we see the first man recorded in the Old Testament and forms an important part of history; the beginning of history in fact.

Another historical book, which no one considers to be allegory, poetry, parable or prose, is the book of Acts. The book of Acts is the historical narrative of the birth of the Church in the New Testament. Acts 17: 26 states the following:

*²⁶From one **man** he made all the nations, that they should inhabit the whole earth; and he marked out their appointed times in history and the boundaries of their lands'.* **Acts 17:26**

When reading the epistles, it can also clearly be seen that the Apostle Paul affirms the historical record in the same way the Old Testament does. No one claims St Paul was speaking in mythical language or prose in regard to his statements. The references of the historical nature of the personage of Adam and Eve are therefore well represented throughout the whole of the New Testament.

*²¹'For since death came through a **man**, the resurrection of the dead comes also through a man. ²² For as in **Adam** all die, so in Christ all will be made alive'. (1 Corinthians 15:21-22) (NIV)*

*⁴⁵'So it is written: "The first **man Adam** became a living being"[19]; the last Adam, a life-giving spirit'. (1 Corinthians 15:45) (NIV)*

*³'But I am afraid that just as **Eve** was deceived by the serpent's cunning, your minds may somehow be led astray from your sincere and pure devotion to Christ'. (2 Corinthians 11:3) (NIV)*

*¹³'For **Adam** was formed first, then **Eve**. ¹⁴ And **Adam** was not the one deceived; it was the woman who was deceived and became a sinner'. (1 Timothy 2:13-14) (NIV)*

*⁴⁵'So it is written: "The **first man Adam** became a living being"*⁽ᵃ⁾*; the last Adam, a life-giving spirit. ⁴⁶ The spiritual did not come first, but the natural, and after that the spiritual. ⁴⁷ The first **man was of the dust of the earth**; the second man is of heaven'. (1 Corinthians 15:45-47) (NIV)*

With all the incredible detail the Bible offers from origins, history, law, religious processes, measurements of structures, redemption and prophecies concerning the future; there is no indication at all of any common ancestor with animals. We therefore have complete consistency throughout the whole of the Bible regarding Adam and Eve as historical figures and the first ancestors to have walked in the world, Adam having been made from the dust of the earth. This naturally makes the whole philosophy of picking and choosing what you want to believe very difficult, as you would literally need to remove large portions of the Bible from every section of scripture to fit a particular world view or philosophical narrative. This would look very messy indeed!

It is easy to simply live life and ignore the very principles our own society is even based on. The whole reason why we have a 7-day week, is due to Genesis 1, with God creating the universe and the world in 6 days and resting on the 7th. I thank God for the weekend! All doctrines in the Bible therefore go back to Genesis chapter 1 to 11. If we decide not to adhere to a literalist interpretation of the Bible, then the whole aspect of religious practice becomes nonsensical. If the account of the garden of Eden is a myth, then so is 'original sin'. The mythical story of the Fall would thus nullify the need for sacrifice, redemption, salvation and baptism. Ironically, the denomination that holds the Eucharist at the centre of their faith overturns the idea of the Fall actually having happened as a realistic historical event. If this is the belief, then the ritualistic outworking of the faith would become completely futile.

A simple alteration to doctrine and proclamation of new philosophy regarding scripture based on the interpretation of a word, thereby throwing the rest of scripture out of divine balance, raises some serious questions. The word **'Yom'**, meaning **'day'**, or in some circumstance 'age', needs no different interpretation, especially in the context of the way it is communicated. If non-literalists want to link Darwinism with Genesis, thus throwing in expanses of 'ages' and time based on the word **'Yom'**, then some important considerations need to be made. The word 'Yom', is also used in the 10 commandments, in respect of the day of rest. I am sure we would love to have an 'age' off for the day of rest, but there is no getting around it; 24 hours is the context of the word.

The English language also has words with multiple meanings. If I say: 'my favourite food is a **date**, then I went out on a **date** with my wife. The suit I was wearing on the occasion was a bit **dated**. At least we could both find a **date** that we were both free; then it is unlikely you misunderstood any of the contexts of the word **date** or meaning of the key word. Why does this therefore become plausible with the word 'Yom'?

Placing very careful attention to the word 'day' **(Yom)**, the writer of Genesis traditionally attributed to Moses receiving the word directly from God, throws up some very important repetitions. Please pay close attention to the bold font. The emphasis in Genesis Chapter 1: 1-31 is undeniable:

The History of Creation

1 '*In the beginning God created the heavens and the earth.* *² The earth was without form, and void; and darkness [a] was on the face of the deep. And the Spirit of God was hovering over the face of the waters.*

*³ Then God said, "Let there be light"; and there was light. ⁴ And God saw the light, that it was good; and God divided the light from the darkness. ⁵ God called the light **Day**, and the darkness He called **Night**.* [b] **So the evening and the morning were the first day.**

⁶ Then God said, "Let there be a [c] firmament in the midst of the waters, and let it divide the waters from the waters." ⁷ Thus God made the firmament, and divided the waters which were under the firmament from the waters which were above the firmament; and it was so. ⁸ And God called the firmament Heaven. **So, the evening and the morning were the second day.**

⁹ Then God said, "Let the waters under the heavens be gathered together into one place, and let the dry land appear"; and it was so. ¹⁰ And God called the dry land Earth, and the gathering together of the waters He called Seas. And God saw that it was good.

¹¹ Then God said, "Let the earth bring forth grass, the herb that yields seed, and the fruit tree that yields fruit according to its kind, whose seed is in itself, on the earth"; and it was so. ¹² And the earth brought forth grass, the herb that yields seed according to its kind, and the tree that yields fruit, whose seed is in itself according to its kind. And God saw that it was good. **¹³ So the evening and the morning were the third day.**

[14] Then God said, "Let there be lights in the firmament of the heavens to divide the day from the night; and let them be for signs and seasons, and for days and years; *[15]* and let them be for lights in the firmament of the heavens to give light on the earth"; and it was so. *[16]* Then God made two great [d]lights: the greater light to rule the day, and the lesser light to rule the night. He made the stars also. *[17]* God set them in the firmament of the heavens to give light on the earth, *[18]* and to rule over the day and over the night, and to divide the light from the darkness. And God saw that it was good. *[19]* **So the evening and the morning were the fourth day.**

[20] Then God said, "Let the waters abound with an abundance of living [e]creatures, and let birds fly above the earth across the face of the [f]firmament of the heavens." *[21]* So God created great sea creatures and every living thing that moves, with which the waters abounded, according to their kind, and every winged bird according to its kind. And God saw that it was good. *[22]* And God blessed them, saying, "Be fruitful and multiply, and fill the waters in the seas, and let birds multiply on the earth." *[23]* **So the evening and the morning were the fifth day.**

[24] Then God said, "Let the earth bring forth the living creature according to its kind: cattle and creeping thing and beast of the earth, each according to its kind"; and it was so. *[25]* And God made the beast of the earth according to its kind, cattle according to its kind, and everything that creeps on the earth according to its kind. And God saw that it was good.

[26] Then God said, "Let Us make man in Our image, according to Our likeness; let them have dominion over the fish of the sea, over the birds of the air, and over the cattle, over [g]all the earth and over every creeping thing that creeps on the earth." *[27]* So God created man in His own image; in the image of God

He created him; male and female He created them. ²⁸ *Then God blessed them, and God said to them, "Be fruitful and multiply; fill the earth and subdue it; have dominion over the fish of the sea, over the birds of the air, and over every living thing that [u]moves on the earth."*

²⁹ *And God said, "See, I have given you every herb that yields seed which is on the face of all the earth, and every tree whose fruit yields seed; to you it shall be for food.* ³⁰ *Also, to every beast of the earth, to every bird of the air, and to everything that creeps on the earth, in which there is [u]life, I have given every green herb for food"; and it was so.* ³¹ *Then God saw everything that He had made, and indeed it was very good.* ***So the evening and the morning were the sixth day'.*** *(Genesis Chapter 1: 1-31)*

When reading Chapter 1 of Genesis carefully, it almost seems as if God wrote in a pre-emptive strike to ensure that the validity and historical accuracy and meaning could not be misinterpreted. It is quite evident that you need a lot of help to misunderstand what is written here. Genesis 1 thus forms a chronological account of the creation of the world and universe with God resting on the 7th day. Evening and morning are impossible to interpret in any other way than a 24-hour period, unless you want to venture as far out as singing songs of the dawning of a new 'age'.

The whole theory, that Genesis 2 was written before Genesis 1 based on the evidence presented is also questionable. It is important to state, that Genesis 1 is in chronological order, whereas Genesis 2 is a historical narrative pertaining more to the 6th day in Genesis 1. It fills in the detail, and does not need to be in chronological order. This poses no problem for the full account of creation. The other important thing to consider, is that scripture originally written in Hebrew did not have chapters and verses added until later on, so nit-picking the account based on later additions of numeric organization is also highly questionable. If the numeric chapters and verses were never there in the first place, but added later, the whole theory of two creation accounts falls apart. If we view historical accounts, specifically of non-fiction, it is usually not considered a problem if a chronological account is given with some narrative added later on for more detail and clarity.

Examples of problems identified by non-literalists suggest that Genesis 2:5 throws up an inaccuracy compared with the chronological evidence described in Genesis 1: 11-12:

⁵Before any plant of the field was in the earth and before any herb of the field had grown. For the LORD God had not caused it to rain on the earth, and there was no man to till the ground'; **Genesis 2:5 (NKJV)**

The emphasis would better suggest that God had not yet created bushes or plants in the field before the creation of the first man in verse 7. Vegetation was recorded to have been made on the third day, so what is the explanation for this? The answer for this can easily be found in the same verse. There is no indication that plants had not yet been created, but it is indicated that no one had as yet tilled the ground, neither had some plants yet sprung up. It is the cultivation that is necessary to produce a single harvest or a particular type of crop. God planted the Garden of Eden with trees, and following this event, man went over to agricultural toil. This also relies heavily upon which translation of the Bible you use.

Another issue often thrown up are the activities of the 6th day. According to logical reasoning non-literalists would suggest that it is impossible for Adam to name all the animals on the 6th day and create Eve on the same day. For one, God brought all the animals to Adam to name and they were named as kinds, not individual species of micro-evolution. To keep things short, a cat was a cat, not the various types we have today. It may indeed have been a very busy day, but we do not need to question scripture because of it.

Lastly, questions regarding light, darkness and plant growth may be asked. Plants were created on the 3rd day, whereas the sun and moon were created on the 4th day. The answer to this is quite simple. If light was created on the first day and God is not just the creator, but the sustainer, then this does not become an issue. It is unlikely people will say there cannot be plant life in paradise (heaven), as there is no sun to be seen. The glory of God is likely to sustain and light up everything.

Defending the word of God is not difficult, as it defends itself if it is read in detail and understood. One of the issues evangelicals will have with non-literalist interpretations is regarding the importance of the creation account. If Adam and Eve are not the first human beings, and creation took place according to accepted scientific accounts of the Big Bang and Evolution, where is the design and purpose of God in all this? The Big Bang is sold to us as one big accident, whereas evolution is depicted as un-designed and an unguided process of random mutations bringing forth variety of life in a massively long time-frame. If church teaching suggests we do not literally come from Adam, then it also needs to explain when the animal kingdom crossed over into humanity, especially in view of the dignity of the human person. There is still great emphasis on us being made in the image and likeness of God, yet nullified as a matter of fact. The other question in regard to this, is that that there is no teaching even among non-literalists that suggest animals have a soul and partake in redemption. If humanity comes from the animal kingdom, then at what point did God decide for the soul to enter the body? As mentioned earlier, you need a lot of help to misunderstand what is written. Furthermore, if it isn't broken, why are people trying to dilute it and fix it? The modern-day Church is trying to make the Bible correspond with theories that have only been proven to be fact by dogma and not by actual evidence in any field. At this point you may have decided that some of the suggestions in this book are way off the mark. However, in later chapters we will view the evidence and re-interpret Darwin based on the evidence he actually had available and how we would interpret this evidence in the modern era.

It is worth noting that Evangelicals will not just completely reject the evolutionary theory based on the origins of man, they will also reject George Lemaitre's theory of the Big Bang, as it is completely at odds with Genesis. The big bang idea comes out of explaining the world based on the laws of time and nature, basically naturalism. As explained in the previous chapter, the inventor of this theory **George Lemaître**, a Jesuit priest, kept his religious beliefs and what he called his science clearly separated, saying that his big bang idea left the materialist free to deny God's existence:

> *"As far as I can see, such a theory remains entirely outside any metaphysical or religious question. It leaves the materialist free to deny any transcendental Being... For the believer, it removes any attempt at familiarity with God... It is consonant with Isaiah speaking of the hidden God, hidden even in the beginning of the universe."* (George Lemaitre', The Primeval Atom Hypothesis and the Problem of Clusters of Galaxies, in R Stoops, La Structure et l'Evolution de l'Universe, (1958) 1-32. As translated in Helge Kragh, Cosmology and Controversy; The Historical Development of Two Theories of the Universe (1996) 60)

Of course, the big bang is not operational science (i.e. testable, observable, or repeatable) but historical science (i.e. assumptions about the unobservable past). The big bang *is* really a religion that is used by most astronomers to explain away God. They theorize the universe is 13.7 billion years old.

To conclude this chapter, evangelicals will hold to a literalist view of the Bible for a variety of reasons, most of which I have mentioned above. The key issue with attempting to harmonize Biblical accounts with evolutionary theories poses a big problem, as the order of events are very different than non-literalist would suggest. I will give some examples comparing the order in the Bible and the recorded evolutionary order. In the Bible, matter was created by God. However, in the evolutionary record, matter existed in the beginning. Genesis says the earth was made before the sun and stars: however, evolution would suggest the sun and stars existed before the earth. Ocean before the land versus land before the oceans. Light before the sun, versus sun as the first light shining upon the earth. There was an atmosphere between the hydrosphere in Genesis compared with a contiguous atmosphere and hydrosphere. Land plants before marine organisms, instead of marine organisms as the first life forms. There were fruit trees before fish according to scripture, not fish before fruit trees. Birds were created before the creeping things (insects); however, evolution suggests insects formed before birds. Land vegetation was created before the sun, not the other way around. Birds were made first, then reptiles. Instead evolution suggest reptiles were first. The origins of man account of scripture suggests man was created before woman: however the genetic record suggests woman appeared before man. Modern science says that rain was way before man; however, the Bible states that man was created before rain fell from the sky due to other watering mechanisms in nature. Scripture is clear that the creation process was finished and that it was very good – evolution teachers that the processes of change and adaption are creative processes that are still taking place. The whole account of original sin and man disobeying God is something we know as the Fall, when the whole of creation fell and became corrupted due to man's abuse of free will. Evolution teaches that struggle and death is good, furthermore necessary for the strong to survive. The evolutionary theory is the exact antitheses of scripture and forms everything but an example for Bible-believing Christians to follow. This is why Evangelicals hold the biblical standard.

THE BIBLE AND SCIENTIFIC DISCOVERY

The general view amongst the unchurched, or depending on the heritage of belief, is that the Bible is unscientific i.e. we will just leave the test tubes and the laboratories to the people in white coats. The first chapter of this book however shows us that this could not be further from the truth. It is also fascinating to have a closer look into what the Bible has contributed to scientific understanding of the world. As mentioned before, all science consists of is a body of knowledge, not exclusively disregarding what is written in the world's best seller. Ironically the Bible is the most sold book in the world, unfortunately the least read and probably even less well understood, especially by many who claim to be wise.

There was a time in our history that people thought the earth was piggy-backed on an animal. It was the Bible which gave us the insight, that it was suspended on nothing in space:

"He stretcheth out the north over the empty place, and hangeth the earth upon nothing'. **Job 26:7**

Up until fairly recent history, the Church was convinced the earth was flat. Admittedly, there has been an upsurge in this belief as of late, but the Bible was fast to comment on the form of the earth, even before the famous mathematicians like Pythagoras, or the geographer Eratosthenes, philosopher Aristotle or theologian and astronomer Galileo. Scripture simply states:

"It is He who sits above the circle of the earth." **Isaiah 40:22**

The first law of Thermodynamics also comes into play. This law affirms that neither matter nor energy can be either created or destroyed. There is no creating going on (ex nihilo), neither can anything be fully destroyed. Following creation, the author of Genesis writes:

"Thus, the heavens and the earth, and all the host of them, were finished." **Genesis 2:1**

This verse makes it evidently clear that it was all done i.e. finished, never to be re-started or undone.

The second law of Thermodynamics teaches us that in all physical processes, everything becomes a little less ordered and structured. It is all slowly fading out through wear and tear as energy becomes less potent. This process teaches us that the universe in itself is not eternal and will eventually give of its last. This process is explained to us in Psalm 102: 25-26:

[25] 'Of old You laid the foundation of the earth, And the heavens are the work of Your hands.
[26] They will perish, but You will [a] endure; Yes, they will all grow old like a garment; Like a cloak You will change them, And they will be changed'. **Psalm 102:25-26 (NKJV)**

Up until the 17th century people did not know where all the water went. Thousands of rivers in existence, but little was understood where these bodies of water would disappear to. Something known to us as the hydrologic cycle. The Bible records it so simply, yet it was not fully understood until proven by science:

[6] He who builds His layers[a] in the sky, And has founded His strata in the earth; Who calls for the waters of the sea, And pours them out on the face of the earth— The LORD is His name. **Amos 9:6 NKJ**

'All the rivers run into the sea, Yet the sea is not full; To the place from which the rivers come, there they return again'. **Ecclesiastes 1:7**

'He causes the [a] vapours to ascend from the ends of the earth; He makes lightning for the rain; He brings the wind out of His treasuries'. **Psalm 135:7**

'If the clouds are full of rain, They empty themselves upon the earth; And if a tree falls to the south or the north, In the place where the tree falls, there it shall lie'. **Ecclesiastes 11:3**

Oceanography has always been a fascinating topic. Matthew Maury (1806 - 1873) was considered to be the father of oceanography. He was also a keen student of God's word, as he read Psalm 8:8:

'The birds of the air, And the fish of the sea, that pass through the paths of the seas'. **Psalm 8:8 NKJ**

(Matthew Maury: Photo credit Wikipedia)

Matthew Maury understood the word of God to be literal and sailed the oceans in search for these ocean pathways and found them. He wrote a book on oceanography which is still in print and available today.

There was a time when science believed that the ocean floor itself was flat, yet the Bible had already recorded that the ocean floor contained deep valleys and mountains Jonah 2:6. It was also believed that the oceans were only fed by the rivers and did not contain springs. However Job 38:16 informed us otherwise.

'To the roots of the mountains I sank down; the earth beneath barred me in forever. But you, LORD my God, brought my life up from the pit'. **Jonah 2:6**

[16] Hast thou entered into the springs of the sea? or hast thou walked in the search of the depth'? **Job 38:16**

If we look at the very origins of human life which this book is mainly about, it is difficult to ignore what the Bible tells us in Genesis, that Adam was formed from the dust of the earth, and that God breathed into Adam's nostrils and he became a living soul. Humanity being formed from primordial soup as Darwin suggested is something we will be looking at in greater detail as we dissect what Darwin actually said in the 'Origin of Species'. Could it be that Darwin needs to be re-interpreted? Sir Fred Hoyle, professor of astronomy made the following statement concerning modern thought:

'No matter how large the environment one considers, life cannot have had a random beginning. Troops of monkeys thundering away at random on typewriters could not produce the works of Shakespeare, for the practical reason that the whole observable universe is not large enough to contain the necessary monkey hordes, the necessary typewriters, and

certainly not the waste paper baskets required for the deposition of wrong attempts. The same is true for living material.... The likelihood of the spontaneous formation of life from inanimate matter is one to a number with 40,000 noughts after it.... It is big enough to bury Darwin and the whole theory of evolution. There was no primeval soup, neither on this planet nor on any other, and if the beginnings of life were not random, they must therefore have been the product of purposeful intelligence'. **Sir Fred Hoyle, professor of astronomy, Cambridge University**

(Holye, F. and C. Wickremasinghe. 1984. *Evolution from Space.* New York: Simon & Schuster, 148.)

With this claim in mind, no one can deny the contribution to science Genesis has made concerning the origins of man. The rejection of Darwin's theory of the origins of man is not reserved for creationists alone.

The clarity of the sexes is also very prevalent in the Bible. Male and Female in Genesis and in Matthew 19:4 gives us an insight into the origin and importance of gender.

[4] And He answered and said to them, "Have you not read that He who [a] made them at the beginning 'made them male and female,' [5] and said, 'For this reason a man shall leave his father and mother and be joined to his wife, and the two shall become one flesh'? [6] So then, they are no longer two but one flesh. Therefore, what God has joined together, let not man separate." **Matthew 19:4 NKJ**

This may be ignored as something completely irrelevant, but these early writings show us that life cannot continue without male and female. The one sex is completely dependent on the other. This is why God created a helper for Adam, not just for company, but also for pro-creation. One of the commandments in Genesis was to be fruitful and multiply. All mammals, fish and birds require male and female and this is made clear in the first chapters of the Bible. This poses a problem for evolution, as life is supposed to have originated from a single sex organism, brought to life by a lightning strike as Darwin's warm little pond would have us believe. This gives no answers in regard to complex and complementary reproductive systems. How could life have originated and developed without reproductive systems that complement one another? The Bible has the answers to this, but science is unsatisfied and is attempting to work backwards and find evidence to the contrary. A matter of fact, some scientists are currently trying to push a paradigm, that there is indeed no male or female, i.e. 'you are what you feel you are'.

Claudius Ptolemy was famous for being an astronomer, mathematician and geographer living in the Roman province of Egypt (AD 100 - 170). He wrote the astronomical treatise known as the Almagest. This is the only ancient known surviving treatise on astronomy. Ptolemy catalogued 1100 stars as observable. We now know that there are countless of billions of stars in the universe, with possible 1025 or so which are observable, but cannot be put in a numeric record. The Old Testament prophet Jeremiah already knew this and recorded this fact in the Bible 2500 years ago:

[22]*'As the host of heaven cannot be numbered, neither the sand of the sea measured'.* **Jeremiah 33:22**

Science at one time also believed that all stars were effectively the same until it was discovered that all stars are different. The Bible already had this covered:

[41] *There is one glory of the sun, and another glory of the moon, and another glory of the stars: for one star differeth from another star in glory'.* **1 Corinthians 15:41**

Science also believed that wind blew straight (not in cyclones) and that air was weightless. Scripture told us otherwise:

⁶The wind goeth toward the south, and turneth about unto the north; it whirleth about continually, and the wind returneth again according to his circuits'. **Ecclesiastes 1:6**

²⁵'To make the weight for the winds; and he weigheth the waters by measure'. **Job 28:25**

We find in scripture that blood is the very source of life. There was a very strange practice as recently as a couple of hundred years ago whereby people who were ill were deliberately bled, as the theory suggested that the disease could be released from the body that way. Needless to say, we know now that blood is the very source of life. Many people lost their lives through this medical procedure, whereby science thought they had got it right. The Bible had already made this clear thousands of years before.

'For the life of the flesh is in the blood', **Leviticus 17:11**

The importance of blood and what it actually did was known to the ancients and recorded in the Bible even as far back as Genesis. Circumcision seems like a strange practice to many, however happens in hospitals up and down the country, even for the non-religious for a variety of reasons. It is cleaner and especially healthier for those who live in warmer climates to avoid infection in the area. The amazing thing to discover is that the command for circumcision was a sign of the covenant between God and the Jewish people and needed to take place according to scripture on the 8th day. One might ask why the eighth day is significant. Scientifically, it has now been proven that blood clotting reaches its climax on that day.

[12] *'And he that is eight days old shall be circumcised among you, every man child in your generations, he that is born in the house'.* **Genesis 17:12**

The Old Testament holds countless verses which are scientific marvels, showing the Hebrews how to stay healthy, not just in food laws, but hygiene ones as well. When dealing with disease, it is clear to us today that hands must always be washed under water which is moving, to remove the source of disease in order not to give it a breeding ground. Washing should therefore always take place under running water for the purpose of cleanliness, especially in view of keeping infections at bay in a medical facility. As recently as the 19th century, doctors were still washing their hands in basins of water. This was thought to be a clean environment; however, invisible germs lead to an untold amount of deaths.

In 1845 Doctor Ignaz Semmelweis was shocked by the death rate of women giving birth in hospitals in Vienna. A 30% death rate of women following giving birth was a shocking statistic. Doctor Semmelweis's observation to solving this problem was key, as he took note of doctors handling or examining dead bodies, and then moving on to the ward with pregnant women. This was a time when invisible microscopic diseases were not in the medical books. He then formulated a plan and enforced the rule that Doctors should wash their hands before and after examinations in running water and the results were astounding. The death rate dropped from 30% to just 2%. This principle was well known and recorded in the book of Leviticus thousands of years ago. (Encyclopaedia Britannica)

(Doctor Ignaz Semmelweis: Photo Credit Encylopedia Britannica)

*'And when he that hath an issue is cleansed of his issue; then he shall number to himself seven days for his cleansing, and wash his clothes, and bathe his flesh in **running water**, and shall be clean'.* **Leviticus 15:13**

The Old Testament laws also had it sorted in respect of caring for the sick and dividing the healthy from the sick in the form of quarantining. It took a long time for the field of medicine to discover how crucial separating people with infectious diseases was. The need for it was clear in scripture, furthermore was well understood. Historically we only see the practice of quarantining coming to the forefront as recently as the 17th century. 'It has been calculated that one-fourth to one-third of the total population of Europe, or 25 million persons, **died from plague during the Black Death'**. (Encyclopaedia Britannica) The situation was of course this bad, because the dead and the sick shared the same rooms as the rest of the family. At the time the spread of the disease was blamed on 'bad air', or sometimes the demonic. Had they used the knowledge of the book of Leviticus, the situation could have been brought under control much quicker.

[46]'All the days wherein the plague shall be in him he shall be defiled; he is unclean: he shall dwell alone; without the camp shall his habitation be'. **Leviticus 13:46 (KJV)**

(The Black death: Photo Credit Encyclopedia Britannica)

Creation: On the Origin of Man

Scientifically there is also much to be said for the benefit of Kosher eating. Jewish food eating laws have always been seen as being a bit extreme, but on closer inspection we would need to see what is banned under the food eating laws. The book of Leviticus was clear concerning what the people were allowed to eat in the hot climate and what was actually banned. It is not difficult to work out why God banned these foods for the Hebrews when the law was given in the desert. Verses 1-23, may seem long, but all will be revealed why this was important.

'The LORD spoke to Moses and Aaron, [2]"Tell the Israelites: Here are the kinds of land animals you may eat: [3]all animals that have completely divided hoofs and that also chew their cud. [4]However, from those that either chew their cud or have divided hoofs, these are the kinds you must never eat: You must never eat camels. (Camels are unclean because they chew their cud but do not have divided hoofs.) [5]You must never eat rock badgers. (Rock badgers are unclean because they chew their cud but do not have divided hoofs.) [6]You must never eat rabbits. (Rabbits are unclean because they chew their cud but do not have divided hoofs.) [7]You must never eat pigs. (Because pigs have completely divided hoofs but do not chew their cud, they are also unclean.) [8]Never eat the meat of these animals or touch their dead bodies. They are unclean for you.
[9]"Here are the kinds of creatures that live in the water which you may eat—anything in the seas and streams that has fins and scales. [10]However, you must consider all swarming creatures living in the seas or the streams that have no fins or scales disgusting. [11]They must remain disgusting to you. Never eat their meat. Consider their dead bodies disgusting. [12]Every creature in the water without fins or scales is disgusting to you.
[13]"Here are the kinds of birds you must consider disgusting and must not eat. They are eagles, bearded vultures, black vultures, [14]kites, all types of buzzards, [15]all types of crows,

[16] *ostriches, nighthawks, seagulls, all types of falcons,* [17] *little owls, cormorants, great owls,* [18] *barn owls, pelicans, ospreys,* [19] *storks, all types of herons, hoopoes, and* **bats**.
[20] *"Every swarming, winged insect that walks across the ground like a four-legged animal is disgusting to you.* [21] *However, you may eat winged insects that swarm if they use their legs to hop on the ground.* [22] *You may eat any kind of locust, cricket, katydid, or grasshopper.* [23] *Every kind of winged insect that walks across the ground like a four-legged animal is disgusting to you'.* **(Leviticus 11: 1-23)**

You may be wondering what the point of all that was, but scientifically we now know the health implications of eating these creatures, especially in a hot climate. All creatures mentioned on the food ban are high in parasites. To set the record straight, to kill all the parasites in pork, you need to grill the chop to the size of a biscuit to deal with all the microbes in the meat properly. Furthermore, we now know that all shell fish or fish without scales or fins are likely to be ocean bottom cleaners, will scavenge and eat excrement to purify the water. All high in unhelpful microbes.

Examples of food permissible to be eaten according to Kosher food eating instructions are listed below, as they do not fall under the forbidden list:

- Livestock - cow, deer, lamb, buffalo, elk, goat, moose
- Fish - bass, bluefish, crappie, perch, pike, salmon, sunfish, trout
- Birds - chicken, pheasant, grouse, quail
- Insects - locusts, crickets, grasshoppers

To add to this, there are specific parts of the body of these animals that are also not allowed to be consumed. Certain non-kosher animal parts, like the tail, the sciatic nerve and some fats generally found in the hindquarters, are separated for obvious reasons. Experts say the benefit also of Kosher eating is because all kosher meats are thoroughly salted, therefore, may be less likely to carry E. coli and salmonella. The separation of meat and dairy also safeguards against cross contamination. God knew these foods were not advised for the Hebrews in the climate they were living in, something we scientifically have only got to grasp with in recent history. I am not suggesting we all eat Kosher, but I am making the point that healthy diet was recorded for a reason that we are only able to now to scientifically understand, especially during a time when there is much concern regarding processed foods, contaminants, genetically modified produce and an upsurge of allergies. The Corona Virus, Covid 19 has been traditionally attributed to the eating of bats and rats, all outlawed by the book of Leviticus.

Something I frequently encounter amongst students when I explain the scriptural past is always: 'What about the dinosaurs'? Science today suggests that homo-sapiens never walked the earth with the dinosaurs. It is ingrained in every student's mind from the most elementary science lessons. It is important to point out that the word dinosaur originates from 1842 onwards. In the book of Job, God is describing two specific creatures to Job, creatures that he is evidentially aware of. One called Behemoth and the other Leviathan. I will deal with the Behemoth in detail as it appears first in scripture:

"Look now at the [a]behemoth, which I made along with you; He eats grass like an ox.
[16] See now, his strength is in his hips, And his power is in his stomach muscles.
[17] He moves his tail like a cedar; The sinews of his thighs are tightly knit. [18] His bones are like beams of bronze, His ribs like bars of iron.[19] He is the first of the ways of God; Only He who made him can bring near His sword. [20] Surely the mountains yield food for him,

And all the beasts of the field play there. ²¹ *He lies under the lotus trees,*
In a covert of reeds and marsh. ²² *The lotus trees cover him with their shade;*
The willows by the brook surround him. ²³ *Indeed the river may rage, yet he is not disturbed;*
He is confident, though the Jordan gushes into his mouth, ²⁴ *Though he takes it in his eyes,*
Or one pierces his nose with a snare'. **Job 40:15-24 (NKJV)**

Points to glean from this scripture, was that it was clearly a very large creature, it was incredibly strong and it had a tail the size of a tree. Cedars are known as one of the biggest trees in the middle east. The bones of the creature were as strong as iron and it lived amongst the trees and marshes, yet cannot be moved by the strong currents of rivers, neither can it be caught by a snare. The Jordan can gush into its mouth, indicating that it can drink large volumes of water. This describes nothing we know today. From the descriptions available, it is likely to be a herbivore dinosaur of some description. A dinosaur that is not concerned by the appearance of a sword.

The second mystery sea creature is the Leviathan described in **Job 41-34**. This scripture is too long to quote, but it is a very detailed description of a sea creature. A fierce beast, which is unable to be killed by harpoons or fishing spears. It is a completely invincible creature with double armour that cannot be tamed. We cannot specifically identify scientifically which beast is being described here, but it is unlikely to still be around today. The book of Job is set in the same era as the book of Genesis, which indicates that the time frame is closer to the beginning of time. Aside from the Bible, descriptions of dinosaurs can be confirmed by the father of History Herodutus and the Jewish historian Titus Flavious Josephus, or even ancient Chinese history.

Speaking of reptiles, it was only till fairly recent history that it was discovered that snakes used to have legs (National Geographic 2016). The book of Genesis confirms that serpents used to have legs in the 3rd chapter.

^{14}'So the LORD God said to the **serpent:** *"Because you have done this,*
You are cursed more than all cattle, And more than every beast of the field;
On your belly you shall go, And you shall eat dust All the days of your life.
^{15}And I will put enmity, Between you and the woman, And between your seed and her Seed;
He shall bruise your head, And you shall bruise His heel'.
Genesis 3:14-15 (NKJV)

To a large extent science had been ignorant of the existence of invisible elements such as atoms, until more sophisticated technology had been developed to study atoms and particles. The Bible already pointed out these elements in Hebrews:

^{3}Through faith we understand that the worlds were framed by the word of God, so that things which are seen were not made of things which do appear'. **Hebrews 11:3**

We are living in a time when belief in the Bible is downgraded to legends and myths, but considering the vast amount of wisdom identified in this chapter on a scientific level, these claims are largely down to ignorance of existing historical records of old, rather than well researched evidence of historical science. It is true these evidences are not recent and how could they be, but many of the points made above do confirm, that what was considered to be evidence-based science many a time, failed to recognise what was already established firmly in the word of God. I think this is also where the definition of the word 'science', once more comes to the forefront as indicated in the previous chapter. **Augustine** defined science as: 'anything to do with knowledge of the temporal world'. **Thomas Aquinas** considered theology a science because it encounters 'special and general revelation'.

EVOLUTION AND THE ORIGINS OF LIFE

Many people consider it important to view Darwin's work in proportion to the era he lived in and the discoveries made during that century. The 19th century marked a period of literary success; one book which especially comes to mind is taught in many schools for the purpose of English exams. Frankenstein is a novel written by British author Mary Shelly about the eccentric scientist Victor Frankenstein, who creates a monster in an unorthodox scientific experiment. This novel was published in 1818. This is just another example of matter colliding with energy leading to consciousness. It is a novel which comes under the fiction category of the library. Man, even with all scientific advances today has been unable to bring anything to life or consciousness on purpose, let alone by random chance, even if the biological matter was available.

It is this mystical force of electricity in the 19th century that sparked the imagination. This era marked some groundbreaking discoveries in the field of science. It was this time when science was being birthed as a belief system and the discovery of electricity left no boundaries for future possibilities. It was the century in which Charles Darwin sailed on the Beagle in 1831 and in 1835, making interesting discoveries concerning micro evolution with turtles and finches in the Galapagos Islands. The locals were able to tell which tortoise came from certain islands and that each island was perceived to have different species of finches. He concluded that all the finches on the islands needed to have originated from an original couple of finches. After his many observations and further conclusions of the survival of the fittest his first work 'On the origin of species', was published in 1859.

There has never been a published scientific work that has shaped the world into a streamlined view, permeating the way we perceive the physical, biological and psychological sciences. Darwin's book has not just been confined to these fields, but has affected decisions made in history and more recently Christian Theology as well.

What caused this ripple effect of Darwin's book? What did he claim that made any budding scientist's head spin with joy? It was through Darwin's book that we saw an alternative belief system develop that challenged the account given to us in scripture. He didn't specifically give an explanation regarding the origin of life itself, which one would have thought he would have done given the title of his book, but he did theorize a theory in a letter to a friend. Microscopes were not particularly powerful in those days; however, it did not seem unreasonable to assume that life itself could have emerged by a chance combination of a variety of chemicals.

'But if we could conceive in some warm little pond, with all sorts of ammonia and phosphoric salts, light, heat, electricity.... present, that a protein compound was chemically formed ready to undergo still more complex changes'. (Letter sometimes dated 1871, Darwin to Charles Hooker dated March 29, 1863)

He was cautious in his approach to the subject of the origin of all life; however, spontaneous chemical generation was indeed the theory he was leaning towards. It was Thomas Huxley who enthusiastically developed the theory relating to primordial slime, then before long by the development of others, the biology text books we all had in school reflected the idea of the primordial soup and Darwin's warm little pond. This was not presented as theory, but as fact.

The complexity of the cell was only realised in the latter stage of the 20th century: furthermore, the probability of life evolving from nothing was becoming less likely with this discovery. It is only later on that the Russian chemist Alexander Oparin really decided to tackle the issue of the origins of life. The formation of the first cell through random chance of chemicals changing over very large periods of time became Oparin's obsession and was further developed by the famous experiment by Stanley Miller in 1953. This was the confirming experiment that led many a person to become an atheist, as it supposed that life could have started by a mixture of chemicals and energy. Before, however, commenting on this experiment, it may be useful to ascertain what constitutes an acceptable scientific theory. It is rational to conclude that a scientific theory is a careful attempt to explain certain observable facts of nature by means of experimentation. A theory must therefore be observable, must be repeatable and must be testable. We can only call a scientific theory true, if it has passed the rigours of scientific observation by repeated experiments. A scientific theory can be called such, if it follows the lines of a well substantiated idea of some aspects of natural world that include facts, laws, inferences and tested hypotheses. The twentieth century's rendition of Darwin's warm little pond can be visually imagined by energy colliding with the primordial soup to produce the first living cell. The question however is, can matter and energy create organic life?

The 1953 'origins of life experiment', by Stanley Miller allegedly at first did just that. He managed to produce primitive amino acids, by recreating what he envisaged to be the primordial soup consisting of methane, ammonia, hydrogen and water vapour. Primitive amino acids, however, were a far cry from the first living cell and in the 1960s this theory was reviewed by geo-chemists as they realised that hydrogen would have escaped this whole process. The experiment was repeated by Stanley Miller this time with just carbon dioxide, nitrogen and water vapour. The results were disappointing for him, as they concluded with no development of primitive amino acids.

(Origins of Life Experiment: Photo credit: latimes.com)

Even if it were possible under these conditions, the question as a direct consequence has to be asked, whether primitive acids dissolved in the ocean can give you a living cell. Biologist Jonathan Wells from the Discovery Institute of the University of California does not seem to think so. His reasoning is as follows:

'If you create a perfect environment for a living cell in a test-tube to survive and place a living cell inside, then take a sterile needle and puncture it, all the molecules leak out of the cell.

After this, you will not be able to make a living cell out of these molecules. You cannot put Humpty Dumpty together again. You are still millions of miles from creating a living cell. There is no theory that has finalized how basic chemical components could have arranged themselves into the first living cell'. (Jonathan Wells)

It is evident from Wells above, that even by creating a perfect environment, the claims made, even by mixing in immeasurable periods of time, a single cell is not going to develop and proclaiming this to be a fact is completely devoid of realism. It is not observable, successfully testable or repeatable. Wells is not the first scientist to come to this conclusion. Jeffrey Tompkins has also made the following observation:

'The main problem regarding false ideas about protein evolution is one of perception associated with the steady diet of academia's evolutionary false teachings'.
(Jeffrey Tomkins (Ph.d Genetics), Engineered Protein Evolution, Proves Biological Complexity', Acts and Facts, March 2013)

Physicist Hubert Yockey has also come to similar conclusions:

'A great deal of effort has been expended in finding theories for the origin of life without success'.
(Hubert Yockey (Ph.D. Physics), Information Theory, Evolution, and the Origin of life, 2005, p. 188)

Even Stanley Miller who initially through his origins of life experiment converted many to Atheism admitted in 1991:

'The origins of life has turned out to be much more difficult than I, and most other people, envisioned'.

(Horgan, 'In the Beginning', Scientific American, Vol 264 p 100-109, 2 Feb 1991)

One may think that I am being selective in mainly quoting biased scientists who seem to have a gripe with the concept of evolutionary theory or teachings. I will, therefore, attempt to balance out the evidence. If there has ever been a scientist in recent history excited about evolution, it would have to be Richard Dawkins. He has indeed been the cover-boy of the century in regard to evolution, almost in an evangelistic way. His admissions, however, seem to verify the above dilemma:

'The theory we seek, of the origin of life on this planet, should therefore positively not be a plausible theory'!
(Richard Dawkins (Ph.D, Professor of Zoology), The Greatest Show on Earth: The Evidence for Evolution, 2009, p. 422.)

A couple of years before Richard Dawkins made this statement in regard to the possibility of the theory of evolution being a plausible theory, he had an interview with Ben Stein and was asked the following questions:

Ben Stein: *Well then who did create the heavens and the earth?*

Prof Dawkins: *Why do you use the word 'who'? You see you immediately beg the question by using the word 'who'.*

Ben Stein: *Well then how did it get created?*

Prof Dawkins: *Well, um, by a very slow process.*

Ben Stein: *Well how did it start?*

Prof Dawkins: **Nobody knows how it started.** *We know the kind of event that it must have been. We know the sort of event that must have happened for the origin of life.*

Ben Stein: *And what was that?*

Prof Dawkins: *It was the origin of the first self-replicating molecule.*

Ben Stein: *Right and how did that happen?*

Prof Dawkins: *I've told you, we don't know.*

Ben Stein: *So you have no idea how it started.*

Prof Dawkins: **No, no, nor has anyone.**

Ben Stein: **Nor has anyone else.**

Ben Stein: *What do you think is the possibility that Intelligent Design might turn out to be the answer to some issues in genetics or in Darwinian evolution?*

Prof Dawkins: *Well it could come about in the following way. It could be that, eh, at some earlier time somewhere in the universe a civilization evolved by probably **some***

	kind of Darwinian *means to a very, very, high level of technology and designed a form of life that they seeded onto perhaps this planet. Ehm, now, that is a possibility and an intriguing possibility and **I suppose it's possible that you might find evidence for that if you look at the um detail, details, of biochemistry, molecular biology, you might find a signature of some sort of designer.***
Ben Stein:	*(Voiceover narration) Wait a second, Richard Dawkins thought Intelligent Design might be a legitimate pursuit.*
Prof Dawkins:	*Um..and that designer could well be a higher intelligence from elsewhere in the universe.*
Ben Stein:	*But, but*
Prof Dawkins:	*But that higher intelligence would itself have had to have come about by some explicable, or ultimately explicable process, he couldn't have just jumped into existence spontaneously, that's the point.*
Ben Stein:	*(voiceover narration) So Professor Dawkins was not against Intelligent Design, just certain types of Designers,* ***such as God.***

Well, there you have it – *'if you look at the details of biochemistry, molecular biology, you might find a **signature** of some sort of **designer**…and that designer could well be a higher intelligence from elsewhere in the universe'*. In a nutshell, that's Intelligent Design. (Stein 2008)

This interview statement by Richard Dawkins is intriguing, in that he views people who even believe in Intelligent Design as relatively lacking in common sense or not worthy of being taken seriously. However, with all the travelling and evangelising the gospel of Darwin, he makes a number of shocking admissions. His first admission, is that no one knows how life originally started, although speaking of the origin of the first self-replicating molecule; furthermore confirming for a second time that no one knows how life began. This is simply not Darwinian and a highly unlikely response you would expect from a person everyone has championed as a hero for atheistic evolution. To add another truth bomb, he then suggests that life could have originated due to some sort of signature of a designer from a civilisation somewhere out in the universe, not to forget of course by some kind of Darwinian means. This is when speculation and science fiction combined becomes a plausible theory based on who is speculating. Stein is rightly quick to point out that Dawkins has effectively snookered himself by admitting clear references to intelligent design and a designer. This is the teleological theory presented in perfection. If it is designed, then there is a designer and the designer must be God!

If we carefully look at the admissions of scientists, it is clear that the same questions still exist today as they did whilst Darwin was still alive. It is also evident that it is unlikely any scientists actually believe in evolution the way Darwin had first envisaged. So, what we have instead is a form of Neo-Darwinism that only identifies with certain points of Darwinian evolution. It is ironic that over 150 years, reality tells us that no progress in any field of scientific endeavour has managed to supply us with any explanation whatsoever concerning the origins of life. Scientists will spend many years qualifying in a particular field of micro study and then impose a particular 'world view' on that micro study. Doctor John Lennox from Oxford University makes the interesting point, that instead of science forming a 'world view', the opposite takes place, in that biases in our own 'world view', effectively dictate our science (Stein 2007). To add to this micro study of the world we then have this narrow sliver of discovery taking on a philosophical form. Einstein was quick to point out the dangers of this approach:

'The man of science is a poor philosopher'. **Albert Einstein** (Albert Einstein (2016). "The Albert Einstein Collection: Essays in Humanism, The Theory of Relativity, and The World As I See It", p.116, Open Road Media)

It is important to note, within Darwinian evolution, the origins and development of life theory relies completely on an undirected process, completely devoid of any design, purpose or plan, thus making it incompatible with a creator. Darwin believed that a cell was a simple blob of protoplasm as did all the scientists of his era. Biochemist Michael Behe highlights the dilemma of irreducible complexity as he points out what the cell evidentially is like, in the form of a bio molecular machine. Machines are designed and are not a result of a random chance existence. One example of this is the Bacterial Flagellum which has an outboard motor. It is not possible that anything like this could come about without any foresight or plan. (Biochemist Michael Behe, Lehigh University) Professor Andy McIntosh inform us that a further example of design is the ATP motor, which produces energy in every living cell (Professor of Thermodynamics, University of Leeds). A very important question to ask, therefore is whether the discovery of biological machinery today can be explained away by Darwinian processes? We will deal with this in out next chapter.

SMALL SUCCESSIVE MUTATIONS

Many years ago, as with most children and young adults, I had a fascination with computer games. Progress toward quality graphics or uploading time was however painfully slow. The digital age of programming was upon us. Earlier versions of IT required you to play a tape in the deck of the computer to download the game for 45 minutes. Things then sped up when the digital information was downloaded via a floppy disk. I remember with excitement when I was able to play a game on my friend's computer, that he had completely programmed himself following days and days of programming from the manual. Days and days of just sitting there and inputting information to be able to play a very standard game in blocks which effectively repeated the same motions again and again. It was simple, yet gripping, especially since the arcade required a lot of coins to enjoy only moments of fun. The horror stories from some of the other children in school also emerged, in that they also spent hours and hours inputting the all-important programming data only to come to the end of their tiring journey, not to have the game load. What was the malfunction to the loading of the eagerly anticipated game with poor graphics? One of the multiple thousands of digits typed in during the programming may have been wrong, skipped entirely or not typed in the desired format. This spelled disaster for the creation and loading of the product resulting in a non-event. It was a micro piece of information that was either wrong, or missing from the puzzle in the grand scheme of things. You may be wondering why I am telling this story, as this book is not really related to the frustrations of the development of computer science: however, the link does evidentially become clear.

In a previous chapter we were dealing with the alleged self-replicating molecules in the form of the first living cell, yet to be proven beyond a shadow of a doubt. DNA is a very long chain of molecules that also requires digital information for the function of the cell. It is coded in four letters almost forming an infinitely long sentence. The segments of DNA appear in two strands that need to complement each other in order to replicate. To put things simply, if they do not complement each other with perhaps 3 billion pieces of information needing to appear in an exact order, then no replication takes place. This of course does not allow for mistakes. Macro evolution takes things even a step further. It requires mutations bringing about new pieces of information to bring about a change. The theory of evolution relies completely on this concept. This would be a change in DNA, which is effectively the hereditary material of life. DNA affects everything from behaviour, to its appearance and physiology. It is the change in an organism's DNA that alters all aspects of its life, which is called a mutation. Darwinism therefore relies completely on small successive mutations altering structures to new forms and species. In other words, without mutation evolution cannot take place. These are considered to change from generation to generation.

I think at this point it is important to ascertain what Darwin effectively said about his own theory in regard to small changes taking place in 'On the Origin of Species'.

> *'If it could be demonstrated that any complex organ existed, which could not possibly have been formed by numerous, successive slight modifications my theory would absolutely break down'.* (Darwin 1859)

It is evident that Darwin's theory revolves completely around the absence of any type of design of biological machinery or coding sequences of DNA. Aspects of design cannot be explained away by naturalistic means.

(Darwin: Photo credit: Pinterest)

In many respects one may actually wonder if he managed to negate his own theory by this one sentence. It is however evidentially true that it is mainly his successors that popularized the idea of small successive mutations being possible in macro evolution. The small successive changes within species in the form of micro evolution no one argues with as the genetic information allows it. One only needs to take the example of the bull finches' beaks, or wolves being domesticated to see micro evolution in process. However, they are clearly defined as within their own species or kind.

Micro evolution is explained easiest within dogs. It is evident in all form of dogs, but it is clear that it is the wolf (common ancestor) at the top of the DNA chain that possesses all the genetic information necessary to breed down to a Chihuahua. There is no miracle possible to use the lack of DNA information in the Chihuahua to breed back up to the wolf, as large portions of the DNA information have now been lost. This is also the precise problem with the theory of macro evolution being a possibility. In natural selection it is only possible to take from the genetic information which is already available, not from new genetic information that is clearly not there. This is why it is not possible to observe one species turn into another: neither is it evident in the fossil record.

All biology text books include the existence of something called the tree of life illustrating a common ancestor. It may even include a chart of an upward progression of species in the form of a geological time-scale. Darwin's book 'On the Origin of the Species', only alludes to a single illustration of this idea.

Creation: On the Origin of Man

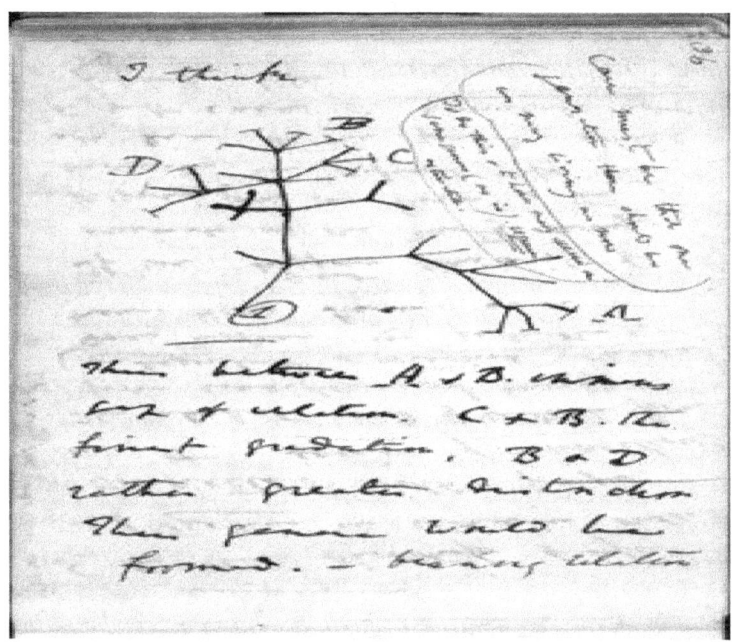

(Darwin's Tree Map: Photo credit: Wikipedia)

The tree map, or even thinking map by Darwin's hand if you would like to label it as so, does not represent the bio-diverse intensity illustrated in the theories we attribute to Darwin. Furthermore, with all the progress of analysis we have available to us now, we still cannot conclusively put our finger on the clear evidence to the origin of all life. Evolution requires small successive mutations to be validated, yet the evidence available to us is to the contrary. It requires the idea of endless new genetic information appearing from nowhere, from the first replicating cell to the development of the sexes and the immense biodiversity we have today in all shapes and sizes. The following are some observational quotes that question this paradigm.

'*The typical mutation is very mild. It usually has no effect, but show up as a small decrease in viability or fertility. Each mutation leads ultimately to one genetic death'.*

(James Crow, Professor of Genetics, University of Wisconsin, 1997)

"*DNA is an information code. The overwhelming conclusion is that information does not and cannot arise spontaneously by mechanistic processes. Intelligence is a necessity in the origin of any informational code, including the genetic code, no matter how much time is given.*"

(Lane Lester (Ph.D, Genetics) and Ray Bohlin (Ph.D. Molecular and Cell Biology), The Natural Limits to Biological Change, 1989, p 157.)

"*But in all the reading I've done in the life-sciences literature, I've never found a mutation that added information.*"

(Lee Spetner (Ph.D. Physics), John Hopkins University, Not By Chance, 1997, pp. 131,138)

"*It seems fair to point out that evolutionists have yet to provide even a single concrete example of a mutation leading to an increase of information as requested.*"

(Royal Truman (Ph.D. Chemistry) The Problem of Information for the Theory of Evolution', 2002, p. 14.)

'*About 4 in 10,000 of known mutations are presumed to be beneficial. However, these are only beneficial in a very narrow sense since they involve a loss of function. Not one of these mutations unambiguously created new information'.*

(Jerry Bergman, Ph.D. Human Biology, Research on the Deterioration of the genome and Darwinism: Why mutations result in the degeneration of the genome, 2004)

To put things in a nutshell, the rules of probability come into play massively. These probabilities are calculated in the likelihood of related mutations. 2 related mutations are put in the realm of 1 in 100 trillion. 3 related mutations are estimated as one in a billion trillion. Four related mutations I cannot even get on the page. The name of the game on behalf of the evolutionist is then to suggest: 'So, you are saying that there is still a chance'?

In conclusion it is also important to know the difference between mutations and simply new traits emerging based on the genetic information that was already available when genes switch on and off. This is characterized in different patterns of an animal's fur, or cats not having a tail, furthermore different eye colour. The small successive mutations Darwin was likely to have been pointing towards were higher levels of functioning. As we have discovered, there is no evidence available pointing toward an upward evolutionary process, rather observations of genetic death. The genome was not something Darwin had envisaged, especially the realms of impossibility to produce one randomly.

Creation: On the Origin of Man

MISSING LINKS

The word ancestor is of course the word that most of us cling to with great interest. We want to know our origins; we want to also know where we come from. This is what generates the interest in ancestry websites and the need to know who our fore-fathers were, what they did and how they behaved. This is when the old family photo albums become interesting and the stories that are told by family who are still alive. It is this cornerstone that gives us meaning and the possible longing for a privileged past. It is within these foundations that we define ourselves, or on the contrary choose to make a change for the better. Ancestry is however a limiting factor, in that one eventually stumbles upon the end of the record, that picture or document that wasn't passed down, that name change or incomplete record at the registry office. In the case of the Bible however, the genealogy records are complete, all the way from Jesus back to Adam in Luke chapter 3. The Jews were meticulous record keepers. Scribes would not just copy: they did things in a mathematical process, counting even letters on lines triple checked by other scribes. To the Bible believing Christian, there is of course no missing link. The picture is complete and does not form a gap filling exercise to fill in the blanks. The discovery of truth is therefore manifest in not just reading God's word, but also studying it.

For others, belief in the origins of man being created in the image and likeness of God on a literal basis can only progress by viewing life through a laboratory test tube. This is where the study of Y-Chromosomal Adam and Mitochondrial Eve enters the stage. "Y-Chromosomal Adam" and "Mitochondrial Eve" are the scientifically-proven theories that every man alive today is descended from a single man and every man and woman alive today is descended from a single woman. They concluded that humanity must have

experienced a genetic bottleneck in the past, which may not have been as infinitely far back as many would like to suggest. Further to their study, it was found that every man alive today actually descended from a single man whom scientists now refer to as "Y-Chromosomal Adam." Mitochondrial Eve is believed to be the mother of all living humans, male and female.
(Dorit, R.L., Akashi, H. and Gilbert, W. "Absence of polymorphism at the ZFY locus on the human Y chromosome." 1995)

It is difficult for evolutionists to deny the above. However, there will be discrepancies in regard to whether these original humans lived at the same time according to different scientific studies. These would, however, likely be assumptions rather than fact. The timeframe within the parameters of Darwinian thought is of course very different from the Biblical view. One truth we can derive from the study is; that every man today is descendant from one man, and every human alive is descended from one woman. This also corresponds with scripture:

'And Adam called his wife's name Eve; because she was the mother of all living'. (Genesis 3:20) NKJ

There have been many attempts in evolution to prove the natural selection theory as true. The perfect evidence would be to discover a humanoid that could at least be seen as transitioning to humans we have today. History throws up a number of interesting discoveries that caused a massive ripple of excitement in their time, but have lost their appeal as further evidence has exposed them as outright frauds. This is the very problem evolution has to deal with i.e. it is in constant need of re-inventing itself or at the very least forensically working its way back to finalize the evidence to prove a theory to be true beyond a shadow of a doubt. This doubt you evidentially will not see in the text books. You will just have proclaimed evidence until debunked. Here are a number of examples that may still be used as evidence today, although have been thoroughly discredited over time.

Lucy the chimpanzee. Found in 1974 in Ethiopia by American Paleoanthropologist Donald Johanson. He had a grant to go there to find missing links. When his grant money was in danger of running out, he miraculously found one. The skull was thoroughly crushed, making any analysis quite difficult. Furthermore, the knee joint was found a mile and a half away, 200 feet deeper than the main skeleton. Some museums if they make a display of Lucy include her with human feet, although no feet were found on the fossil. These feet would clearly not be factual. The museums showing an exhibit of Lucy are only fussed about the impression it creates, rather than demonstration of any accuracy. The theory thus becomes more important than the facts. Evolution struggles to blend missing links with today's humans, as ape feet are exclusively designed to climb trees with a big toe more like a thumb sticking out to the side. They can use these to hang from a branch by their back feet. Most experts agree that Lucy was merely a 3-foot chimpanzee. Speaking of chimpanzees, there is a complete lack of fossil evidence as to how these creatures evolved.

Creation: On the Origin of Man

(Lucy – Photo Credit: Cleveland Museum)

Museums put human feet on their exhibits; However aside from evolutionary large expanses of time, some studies do throw up some interesting facts. Russell H. Tuttle discovered some ground-breaking footprints alleged to be 3.5 million years old:

'The 3.5-million-year-old footprint trails at Laetoli site G resemble those of humans. None of their features suggest that the Laetoli hominids were less capable bipeds than we are'.

'If the footprints were not known to be so old, we would readily conclude that they were made by a member of our own genus, homo'. (Russell H. Tuttle, Natural History, March. 1990: p 64 quoted in Bones of Contention, p 174)

With rocks allegedly being infinitely old and footprints that can only have been made from Homo-sapiens believed to be either 200-300 thousand years in age, some would suggest that evolutionary theory is shooting itself in the foot. This pun may indeed be intended.

Heidelberg Man. Constructed from a jawbone that experts decided was actually quite human.

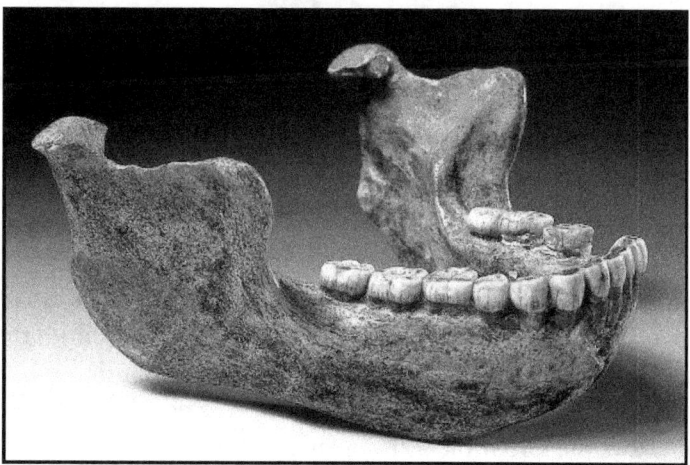

(Heidelberg Man: Photo credit: Gesundindustrie BW)

Nebraska Man: This find was used for years as evidence for evolution. The whole theory of this finding was built around one existing tooth that was later found to be from an extinct pig. Models were creatively put together very imaginatively including the man's partner, based on the one existing tooth.

(Nebraska man and his wife, shown in: illustrated London News 1922).

Piltdown Man: This evidence was allegedly found in Piltdown England, in a gravel pit. After close inspection of this find, the jaw bone was revealed to belong to a modern ape and the skull was human. The ape's jaw had to be filed down to fit. (Encyclopedia Britannica) It was in the text books for 40 years as proof for evolution, but exposed as a fraud in 1953. Now even the local pub that was called 'The Piltdown man', has changed its name to avoid linking itself with a fraud. There is nothing in the area advertising itself with something that at first was considered ground breaking history. (Piltdown Man,

British Archaeologies' greatest Hoax, The Guardian, 4ᵗʰ Feb 2012,)

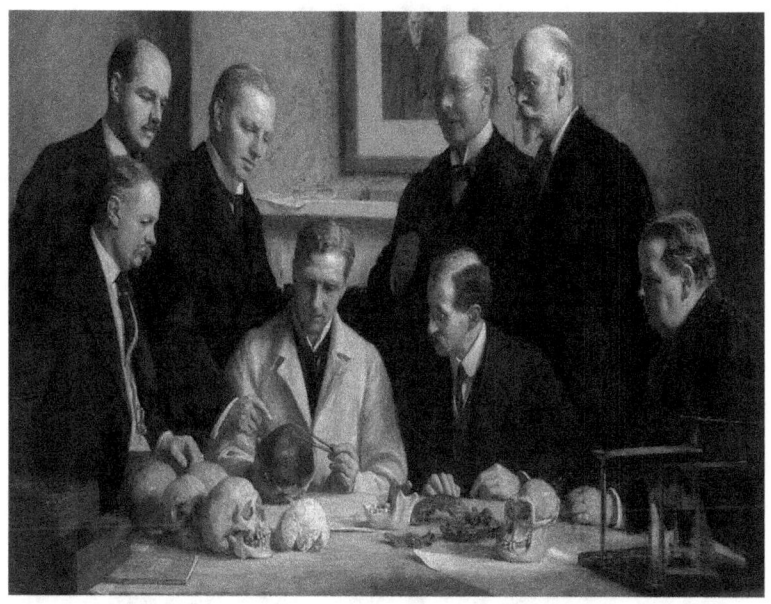

(Piltdown man: Photo Credit: Sciencemag)

Peking Man: When discovered, this man was alleged to have been 500, 000 years old. However, the remains disappeared as quickly as they appeared. The find was from skull fragments found in the 1920s in Peking China. The remains were found in a cave with 10 other humans, including tools. This did not mean the ape was using tools. It means that the humans inside the cave were likely using tools to smash the ape skull to eat its brain. This is a delicacy in some areas of the world. The existence of the remains of 10 humans in the cave was conveniently left out of the record.

(Peking Man: Photo Credit Wikipedia)

Neanderthal Man: This find was discovered in the Neander Valley and was already discredited at the International Congress of Zoology in 1958 by Dr. A.J.E Cave, as the skeleton discovered in France was considered merely to have been a very old man who was suffering from arthritis. This is why he was stooped over. He wasn't stooped over due to transitioning from ape to man and coming up to stand like a human, but rather bending over due to his arthritic condition. The eyebrow ridge in humans never stops growing and protrudes with age, giving the skull a more pre-historic appearance. These are perfectly normal people who have lived to a very old age, which is compatible with the lifespan of people we see in Genesis. Neanderthal man is still in the text books today.

(Neanderthal Man: Photo credit: The Independent)

New Guinea Man: This discovery was in 1970, although the same humans still exist today in a region just north of Australia. Hardly pre-historic.

(New Guinea Man: Photo Credit Pinterest)

Cro-Magnon Man: Considered as one of the earliest discoveries and established fossils in the same league in physique and brain capacity as modern humans. So close in fact, it is difficult to tell the difference.

(Cro-Magnon Man: Photo Credit Wikipedia)

With all the evidences that are presented as missing links, it may be worth looking at the Guinness book of records to discover what record-breaking humans we still have alive today, which do indeed fit descriptions of supposed missing links, varying in height, weight and skull formation. This is not evidence for evolution, merely evidence that occasionally in the past they may have unearthed an unusual human being.

Surprisingly, the hunt for more inclusion of alleged missing links as fact seems to be slowing down, yet the ancestral worship still persists. A verified missing link announced as the final proof of evolution has not emerged in a strong serious capacity for quite a while. Probably due to the fascination of the study of aliens and the possibility of seeding of humanity from another planet, as discussed in one of the previous chapters. Nevertheless, Sir David Attenborough made a fascinating claim in 2009 which was reported in the UK on every news channel and in most papers. This was a coordinated effort even by Google, as it changed its logo on the same day of the announcement to promote this evolutionary discovery. Fossil Ida, extraordinary find is 'missing link', in human evolution was the hypothesis. The evidence was now complete and it would have met the approval of Darwin. Here a quote reported by the Guardian:

'Sir David Attenborough said <u>Darwin</u> "would have been thrilled" to have seen the fossil - and says it tells us who we are and <u>where we came from</u>.
"This little creature is going to show us our connection with the rest of the mammals," he said.
"This is the one that connects us directly with them.
"Now people can say 'okay we are primates, show us the link'.
"The link they would have said up to now is missing - well it's no longer missing."

'Fossil Ida: Extraordinary find is 'missing link' in human evolution, perfectly preserved fossil Ida, unveiled in New York today, provides unprecedented insight into our ancestry'.

(The Guardian Tuesday 19ᵗʰ May 2009)

I have been amazed at Sir David Attenborough's documentaries over a number of years now and no one can argue that he has done a fantastic amount of work for the environment, highlighting the dangers of industrialization, or the dangers of plastic being released into the oceans and food chain. The talk of the finding above, however, disappeared as quickly as it came. The massive news coverage and the trigger words 'approval from Darwin', caused as they always do an enormous amount of interest. When the peer reviews were released it came as no surprise that the fossil seemed to have little difference to ordinary lemurs or lorises. In every sense, it was basically an admission that the link always has been missing, furthermore goes down in history as yet another failed attempt at providing credible evidence. The holy grail of fossils quickly turned into a holy fail of paleontology. This emotional concept is particularly well explained by Holden:

"The field of paleoanthropology naturally excites interest because of our own interest in origins. And, because conclusions of emotional significance to many must be drawn from extremely paltry evidence, it is often difficult to separate the personal from the scientific disputes raging in the field. The primary scientific evidence is a pitifully small array of bones from which to construct man's evolutionary history. One anthropologist has compared the task to that of reconstructing the plot of War and Peace with 13 randomly selected pages. Conflicts tend to last longer because it is so

difficult to find conclusive evidence to send a theory packing." (Constance Holden, "The Politics of Paleoanthropology," *Science*, p.737, August 14, 1981)

In contrast, however, perhaps reconstructing a missing link to serve as a go between for ancestral purposes may be even more difficult, due to the fact that it is based on a fully formed idea founded on an assumption. An idea which has cost untold amounts of money to verify with no success, yet the hunt has persisted for over a century. One might question why DNA has been insufficient to deter further research in something that has no more than emotional significance relating to the desire of confirming a pet theory. Y-Chromosomal Adam and Mitochondrial Eve provide us with the answers we need, but not necessarily the origins most scientists want. Science itself is plagued by the inclusion and rejection of evidence based on a person's pet theory, which we can more or likely agree, usually leans toward attempting to prove evolution in a never-ending paradigm of hype and then disappointment.

Creation: On the Origin of Man

THE FRUITS OF DARWINISM

An important question to ask, is what kind of impact Darwin has had on society. We can only turn to history to give us this answer. Social Darwinism has indeed had a very strong influence on the way people have developed the idea of a human community. If we toy with the ideas of natural evolution and with the notion that species have not been created but came about by random chance, then for the sake of putting humanity in any kind of moralistic framework, then some kind of ethical structure needs to be derived from the process. I am not going to delve too deeply into the question of what morality is, as this is not exactly a philosophical micro study, but it does open up a can of worms when investigating whether more than natural mechanisms are fully operational in nature. Darwinism, therefore, has not just completely changed the way we view science and the world, forming a world view on just science, but rather on the way we view society as a whole. As discussed earlier, Darwinism has framed an approach to viewing life through the lens of a scientific test tube, creating a worldview about the existence of society and not just the forming of a simple scientific hypothesis, or perceived morality.

Dr John G. West addressed this very issue in his book 'Darwin Day in America', as he explains how Darwinian evolution had influenced our entire Western Society, whereas, the theory took the place of the more traditional ways we understood life. This led to massive social and political phenomena in the build up to the second world war. In the 1920s society was looking for solutions to problems in western society, ranging from crime to poverty or even sexual behaviour. They felt at the time that Darwinism could provide some explanations and solutions to these problems. The dangers of these stances on complicated issues resulted in politics and culture being dehumanized, with a complete absence of the sanctity of life. This degrading process reduced humans to no more than biological machines or even animals. The justice system began to suffer the consequences of the lack of existence of 'free will', allowing any punishments to be shelved in favour of lobotomy. Departments of welfare suggested eradicating the economically disadvantaged by sterilization, especially those who were considered as biologically unfit, i.e. viewing people exclusively in economic terms. Business was permeated by racist ideas of human evolution, using advertising methods to influence consumer behaviour. Sexual behaviour was underpinned with a new form of morality, based on animal instincts rather than traditional morality based on the Bible or ethical teachings of the church.

These ideas were developed by biologists and anthropologists in the 1920s. The Nazis themselves were fanatical Darwinists. Aside from the Holocaust itself, 15,000 handicapped people were killed as illness or deformity whether in the body or mind did not fit in with Nazi ethics or eutopia. The Hadamar Euthanasia Centre, known as the "House of Shutters," was a psychiatric hospital located in the German town of Hadamar. Beginning in 1939, the Nazis used this facility as one of six for the T-4 Euthanasia Programme, which performed mass sterilizations and mass murder of "undesirables". These were characterised as members of German society, specifically those with physical and mental disabilities. It at first started with mass sterilizations of children deemed "unfit" to reproduce and pass on their undesirable traits to the next generation. The next step culminated in hospital staff exterminating children determined to be unfit and the programme was later expanded to adults. In the eight months of the first phase of the killing operations 10,072 men, women and children were asphyxiated with carbon monoxide in a gas chamber as part of the Nazi "euthanasia" programme. Thick smoke from the hospital crematorium churned out over the town Hadamar in 1941. The medical staff celebrated the cremation of their 10,000th patient partying with beer and wine. The T-4 programme was top secret: however, the local population seemed to be fully aware of events at the hospital. Local children would taunt one another if a child was not considered particularly clever, pointing out their bleak future. The people murdered there were transported in by train and bus, sometimes up to 100 a day. They were told to disrobe for a "medical examination". They would then be sent to a physician and each was recorded as having one of 60 fatal diseases. People deemed as 'incurables', were to be given a "mercy death."

(Hadamar Euthanasia Centre: Photo Credit: Imperial War Museum)

'The doctor identified each person with different-coloured sticking plasters for one of three categories: kill; kill & remove brain for research; kill & extract gold teeth'. (Patrizia Barbera: *Todgeweihte kamen in Postbussen zur Hinrichtung*, in *Frankfurter Allgemeine Zeitung,* page 55, 21 October 2008)

Since the crematorium ovens were so busy in this industrial extermination programme, thick smog like smoke remained hanging over the town. It is estimated that at least 200,000 individuals were murdered at these centres, with no holds barred at a person's age. Many of the victims were children carted off to death facilities. It is with great regret that we must consider that people earned themselves Doctorates for taking part in theses atrocities. These actions were in keeping with the eugenics ideas about racial purity developed by German ideologies. While officially ended in 1941, the programme lasted until the German surrender in 1945. Nearly 15,000 German citizens were transported to the hospital and died there, most killed in a gas chamber. In addition, hundreds of forced labourers from Poland and other countries occupied by the Nazis were killed there.

In economic terms, this may have been very much in agreement with a concept developed by the English philosopher Thomas Malthus, who devoted a lot of his time studying population growth and the impact on the economy, especially the tendency of the poor to reproduce more rapidly than other classes in society. Malthus will always be linked to movements relating to population control.

'The ideas of Malthus were a significant influence on the inception of Darwin's theory of evolution.' (Charles Darwin: gentleman naturalist, A biographical sketch by John van Wyhe, 2006)

(Thomas Malthus: Photo Credit Encyclopedia Britannica)

Charles Darwin was convinced by the notion that population growth would eventually lead to more organisms than could possibly survive in any given environment, leading him to theorize that organisms with a relative advantage in the struggle for survival and reproduction would be able to pass their characteristics on to further generations. Proponents of Malthusianism were in turn influenced by Darwin's ideas. These schools of thought influenced the field of eugenics. "humane birth selection through humane birth control" in order to avoid a Malthusian catastrophe by eliminating the "unfit". (Pierre Desrochers; Christine Hoffbauer (2009). "The Post War Intellectual Roots of the Population Bomb")

It naturally comes as little surprise that the full title of Darwin's book in 1859 was titled: 'On the Origin of Species, By Means of Natural Selection, on the Preservation of favoured Races in the struggle for life'. This book cover with the full title has since been modernized with certain words omitted to avoid unnecessary upset.

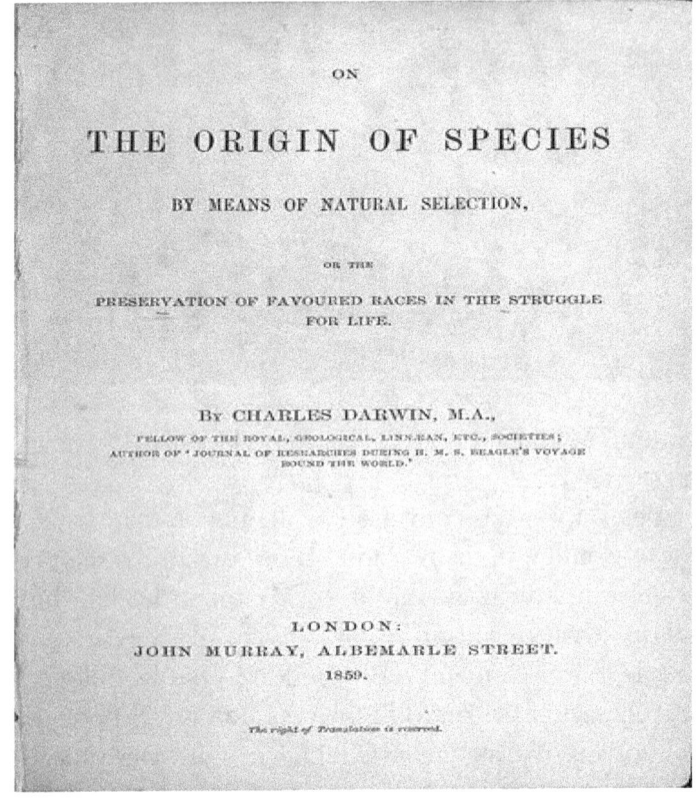

(On the Origin of Species, By Means of Natural Selection, on the Preservation of favoured Races in the Struggle for life, 1859)

The Value of life, or even the sanctity of life is a very important concept in medical ethics. Judeo-Christian ethics consider especially human life to be holy, precious and a gift from God. Dr Richard Weikart in his book 'From Darwin to Hitler', outlines this degrading process of dehumanization which led to mass extermination of 6 million Jews. He explains the revolutionary impact Darwinism had on ethics and morality. This book demonstrated that many leading Darwinian biologists and social thinkers in Germany believed that Darwinism overturned traditional Judeo-Christian ethics, especially the view that human life is sacred. His work demonstrated that many of these thinkers supported moral relativism, yet simultaneously exalted evolutionary 'fitness' to the highest ranking of morality, especially in view of survival of the fittest in health and intelligence. Darwinism played a key role in the rise not only of eugenics, but also euthanasia, infanticide, abortion and racial extermination. This was especially important in Germany, since Hitler built his view of ethics on Darwinian principles, not on traditional morality. (From Darwin to Hitler, Evolutionary Ethics, Eugenics and Racism in Germany, Richard Weikart, Palgrave Macmillan US, 2004)

National Socialism encouraged the sterilization of people who were considered to be feeble minded. How do we characterize eugenics? **Eugenics** is the practice or advocacy of improving the human species by selectively mating people with specific desirable hereditary traits. It aims to reduce human suffering by "breeding out" disease, disabilities and so-called undesirable characteristics from the human population. (Encyclopedia Britannica)

The word "eugenics" was first used in 1883 by the English scientist Francis Galton, who was related to Charles Darwin.

The idea was to promote the utopia of perfecting the human race in a process of exterminating "undesirables" and making sure that those coined "desirables" were multiplied. This is effectively social Darwinism as we know it, by breeding the fit whilst giving nature a helping hand and getting rid of the unfit. The exact science of genetics was not fully understood in Darwin's day: however, the theory of evolution taught that species did change as a result of natural selection and that it would reap many benefits in cattle farming with selected, desirable strong breeds multiplied.

Eugenics in its outset is linked to planned parenthood in the Darwinian struggle for existence. Many people considered Hitler to be insane, but it is quite clear that he was comforted in his science as a provider of a radical solution to the world's problems. He rationalized his science to do evil. He thought he was benefitting humanity by driving his science forward, thereby creating a better humanity. If you read the book 'Mein Kampf', especially in its original German, the radical solutions are clearly there, underpinned by Darwinism. Clearly Darwinism does not automatically equate to Nazism, but if it has been used to rationalize events of the past, what is stopping it from forming events in the future? Abortion, Infanticide and Euthanasia are concepts that seek to rid society immediately of anyone who may be a drain on resources, thinking of people only in economic terms. Effectively, the extermination of individuals can be considered as beneficial in the modern day as organs and other biological matter can be a booming business. Applying Darwinism to humanity at the end of the day, boils down to a devaluing of human life, as the idea of transitioning life forms rids us of the idea of human privilege.

The idea of only allowing the strong to breed is very evident in Darwin's work:

'*With savages, the weak in body or mind are soon eliminated; and those that survive commonly exhibit a vigorous state of health. We civilised men, on the other hand, do our utmost to check the process of elimination; we build asylums for the imbecile, the maimed, and the sick; we institute poor-laws; and our medical men exert their utmost skill to save the life of every one to the last moment. There is reason to believe that vaccination has preserved thousands, who from a weak constitution would formerly have succumbed to small-pox. Thus, the weak members of civilised societies propagate their kind. No one who has attended to the breeding of domestic animals will doubt that this must be highly injurious to the race of man. It is surprising how soon a want of care, or care wrongly directed, leads to the degeneration of a domestic race; but excepting in the case of man himself, hardly any one is so ignorant as to allow his worst animals to breed*'.

(Descent of Man, Darwin 1871)

In the previous chapter I touched upon the number of missing links that have been thoroughly discredited over the years, but I briefly wanted to bring up **New Guinea Man** once again. This discovery was in 1970, although the same humans still exist today in a region just north of Australia, which is hardly pre-historic. If we turn back the clock 100 years from this discovery, the view of people considered to be of lesser value were very evident in Darwin's writings, so much so, indicating a clear future that was envisaged for people considered to be savage races.

"At some future period, not very distant as measured by centuries, the civilized races of man will almost certainly exterminate, and replace, the savage races throughout the world. At the same time the anthropomorphous apes, as Professor Schaffhausen has remarked will no doubt be exterminated. The break between man and his nearest allies will then be wider, for it will intervene between man in a more civilized state, as we may hope, even than the Caucasian, and some ape as low as a baboon, instead of as now between the negro or Australian and the gorilla."

(The Descent of Man Darwin, pp. 200-201)

To discover the impact of just thinking in evolutionary terms over the last century I have clearly used history as the defining factor including the fruits of its inception. One may think I may have been unfair concentrating on the philosophy of Nazism as a natural consequence of completely relying on naturalism. It is therefore very important to note that every government that has adopted a complete atheistic philosophy or has entirely relied on the ethics of Darwinism as the only foundation to explain life, is riddled with the worst human rights abuses known to man. If we look at any other atheistic state, we have the same pattern of devaluing of human life. Stalinist Russia saw 20 million deaths, merely as a result of Stalin's paranoia and need for absolute control. Mau's revolutionist China it is believed caused over 40 million deaths, supposedly for the greater good of humanity and equality. Cambodia suffered the annihilation of a third of the entire population. People were put to death for merely showing possible signs of being able to think for themselves and not part of a communist collective. These are just a few examples without going through an exhaustive list. The holy book becomes the political manifesto of the country and the image to worship is the statue of the dictator. This is why the Bible had been outlawed in all these countries as it directly opposed the ethics of atheistic systems. One would ask oneself how and why people would behave this way, without apparent remorse or fear of consequence. The answer may indeed lie deep in the human psyche; not withholding the fact, that if I don't believe I have come from anywhere, neither am I going anywhere after death without heaven or hell or fear of judgement – then as an autonomous individual a person may feel they can do as they please, especially if it is mainly for the benefit of self. On the reverse side of the coin; if I genuinely believe my origins are linked to the image and likeness of God, and that I have been lovingly created for a purpose and plan, then my actions on earth are more likely to reflect responsibility of accountability.

Creation: On the Origin of Man

SUMMARY

This study started by researching the history of science and who contributed. It was clear that there was not just a significant contribution to science by practising Christians, but rather the actual development of the fields of science we actually know today. These weren't simply legendary scientists, but also many were well regarded theologians. Some associated closely to their denominations and held the Bible in high regard, whereas, for others the Bible stood out as their very foundation for life and belief system. The important aspect we are able to take from this; is that *Science* and *Religion* were not an issue. The workings of their faith did not inhibit their ability to contribute to science; it was actually very much a part of it. The strange concept of defining scientists exclusively as people who interpret the world through a lens of atheism cannot therefore be substantiated by history. The Catholic Church specifically celebrated the following people.

1. St Albert the Great, was a lecturer in theology and made many contributions in a variety of scientific fields. He was made the patron Saint of scientists.
2. Jean Baptiste Lamarck, is credited with pioneering an early form of **evolution** labelled Lamarckism.
3. Gregor Mendel, pioneered genetics; especially famous were his studies of pea plants in the monastery garden in Austria.
4. George Lemaitre, a Jesuit priest and scientist, was the first person to propose the **Big Bang** theory, which is the predominant scientific thought regarding the beginning of the universe till this day.

Non literalist interpretation of the Bible

To review the teachings of the Catholic Church, the Big Bang and the theory of evolution are not seen as compatible with scripture. However, if we take the example of George Lemaitre; he treated his scientific theories and his personal walk with God as something very different. In the 1950 encyclical *Humani generis*, Pope Pius XII confirmed that there is no intrinsic conflict between Christianity and the theory of evolution, provided that Christians believe that God created all things and that the individual soul is a direct creation by God and not the product of purely material forces. Creationists suggest the world was ordered and structured in a period of 6 days according to Genesis 1, whereas evolutionists would suggest, that the order is mostly the same, but the expanses of time are different. What if you stretched the time of Genesis from seven 'days' to seven 'ages' (lengths of time)? After all the Hebrew word for 'day' (Yom) can be interpreted as 'age' in certain circumstances. This could mean the world was formed over a longer (seven ages) period of time, instead of 7 days in Genesis 1.

The Vatican makes it clear that the Magisterium encouraged the importance of both science and religion to be compatible: therefore, mutually supportive following the Second Vatican Council. Catholic scientists are encouraged to use their expertise to assist people grasp the nature and purpose of God's creation. Religion and Science may indeed see issues under a different lens, not through contradiction, but rather due to the diversity of questioning. A main point to be made within Catholicism is that scientific evidence explains the 'how', whereas, religion explores and confirms the 'why', dividing the two truths described earlier as 'scientific truth', and 'theological truth'.

Catholicism in the interpretation of the Genesis accounts, puts caring for the environment as one of the most important principles. This is translated into a New Covenant principle by the following verses and commandments in Mark:

'The first is, 'Hear, O Israel: The Lord our God, the Lord is one; you shall love the Lord your God with all year heart, and with all your soul, and with all your mind, and with all your strength.' The second is this, 'You shall love your neighbour as yourself'. There is no other commandment greater than these'. **Mark 12:29-31**

This again places the emphasis on looking after the environment for many generations to come, therefore, loving your neighbour as yourself. Environmental politics plays a big part, especially in more recent Catholic thought and forms the crux of Catholic belief in regard to the relevance of Genesis, not historical accuracy or a literal scientific account of the origin of humanity. To summarize the teachings of the Catholic Church, the importance or even significance of the Genesis accounts can be put into simple bullet points.

1. We are stewards of Creation.
2. We are made in the Image and likeness of God.
3. Everything that exists was created by God.
4. Everything that God created was good.

Literalist interpretation of the Bible

Many liturgical churches will agree with the perceived liberal interpretation above. This interpretation however does seem very simple, especially if you try and put the whole of the Bible in the actual context it was written. Literalist interpretation of scripture or specifically the book of Genesis could not be more different. Non-literalist reflection of Genesis possibly alludes more to the existence of merely a supreme higher force, rather than the carefully documented evidence brought to us in the Bible. Viewing the 'Creation of Adam' painting by Michelangelo in the Sistine Chapel also represents this notion. In the painting, Adam is brought to life by the touch of God, rather than the forming of the first man from the dust of the earth and God breathing into him life, therefore, becoming a living soul:

⁷And the LORD God formed man of the dust of the ground, and breathed into his nostrils the breath of life; and man became a living soul'. **Genesis 2:7**

Semantics therefore when reviewing scripture in the context it was written, thus becomes very important to the literalist. This is the importance of the Evangelical perception of the origins of man.

Definition of key words naturally become of utmost importance. When we think of "science," we usually think of the study of the natural world and that which can be quantitatively measured—subjects such as biology and physics. Historically though, of the "natural" sciences, only geometry and astronomy were part of the standard university curriculum. So, what was a science? Evangelicals do not separate the concept of having one truth for one thing and another truth for another. Science and theological truth are therefore one and the same thing. I cannot divide your truth, my truth and their truth. There is just one truth: anything else is likely to be just someone else's opinion with all the biases that go along with it. Augustine defined science as: 'anything to do with knowledge of the temporal world'. Thomas Aquinas considered theology a science because it encounters 'special and general revelation'. It is worth noting, that Augustine was more in line with the literal interpretation of the Genesis accounts.

The Bible and a theological standard thus become of utmost importance. Although the scholastic standard has changed in our world, a Christian's belief in biblical inerrancy supports theology as "queen." It is not in the remit of a Bible believing Christian to pick and choose which parts of scripture to include and others to ignore. The Bible warns us to avoid "the opposing ideas of what is falsely called knowledge" (1 Timothy 6:20). Rather, we should strive to "correctly handle the word of truth" (2 Timothy 2:15). Putting scripture in context is of utmost importance. Theology truly is the starting place for learning. "The fear of the LORD is the beginning of knowledge" (Proverbs 1:7).

Evangelical Christians consider Genesis as a true historical and scientific account of the very origin of man, but why? From a literary sense, it therefore becomes important to distinguish between the genres the Bible is written in. When comparing genres of the Bible, one has: historical, poetry, wisdom, prophecy, Gospels (biography & parables) and finally epistles. The grammatical forms of the Hebrew thus become very important as they indicate which genre of writing is taking place. Hebrew uses special grammatical forms for the recording of history, which is the precise forms used in Genesis 1 to 11. This grammatical structure of historical narrative is continued from chapter 12 onwards, into Exodus, Joshua and Judges, which no one suggests is taken as allegory or poetry. The recording of history is the same throughout in those precise grammatical forms. (Steven W. Boyd) The analysis of language is crucial, especially taking close note of who is speaking. If we take Jesus for example, would he really be speaking about a mythical couple when referring to Adam and Eve as a real historical narrative?

*⁴And He answered and said to them, "**Have you not read** that He who [a]made them at the beginning 'made them male and female,'⁵ and said, 'For this reason a **man** shall leave his father*

Creation: On the Origin of Man

and mother and be joined to his wife, and the two shall become one flesh'? **Matthew 19: 4-5**

*⁶But from the beginning of the creation, God 'made them male and female.' ⁷'For this reason a **man** shall leave his father and mother and be joined to his wife, ⁸and the two shall become one flesh'; so then they are no longer two, but one flesh. ⁹Therefore what God has joined together, let not man separate."* **Mark 10: 6-9**

Jesus is not telling a parable; neither is he speaking in allegory or prose. He is recalling an actual factual event which has taken place. The clear reference to Adam as a man does not open up the possibility of referring to a being who has not yet reached that status in the appearance of an ape-like ancestor. There are scores of verses confirming the historical events of Genesis, including Abel, Noah and Lot in the Gospels alone.

Genealogy of course throws up more possibilities for scriptural discussion. Family trees provide interesting reading, whereby people recently have been fascinated researching their own records on ancestry websites, even as far as giving DNA samples to be sent away for analysis. There is nowhere in history, a better and more accurate recording system than that of the Jewish scribes. You may wonder why this is important? The genealogy in Matthew 1 follows the line of Joseph; however traditionally Luke 3 outlines the lineage of Mary, the mother of Jesus all the way back to Adam. The family tree is thus complete, name by name from Adam to Jesus. The Gospel of Luke is also the Gospel outlining Jesus as the perfect Saviour. To suggest these records are fabricated is denying their historical value. The question would then have to be asked again: Which parts of scripture would you agree are factual or entering the realm of mythology? This carefully documents genealogy, of which we see the first man recorded in the Old Testament and forms an important part of history; the beginning of history in fact.

Acts, which no one considers to be allegory, poetry, parable or prose, also records Adam as a literal person. This is the historical narrative of the birth of the Church in the New Testament. Acts 17: 26 states the following:

*²⁶From one **man** he made all the nations, that they should inhabit the whole earth; and he marked out their appointed times in history and the boundaries of their lands'.* **Acts 17:26**

In the epistles we can also see that the Apostle Paul affirms the historical record in the same way the Old Testament does. No one claims St Paul was speaking in mythical language or prose in regard to his statements. The references of the historicity of the personage of Adam and Eve are therefore well represented, throughout the whole of the New Testament.

²¹'For since death came through a **man**, the resurrection of the dead comes also through a man. ²²For as in **Adam** all die, so in Christ all will be made alive'. **1 Corinthians 15:21-22 (NIV)**

⁴⁵'So it is written: "The first **man Adam** became a living being"[a]; the last Adam, a life-giving spirit'. **1 Corinthians 15:45 (NIV)**

*³'But I am afraid that just as **Eve** was deceived by the serpent's cunning, your minds may somehow be led astray from your sincere and pure devotion to Christ'.* **2 Corinthians 11:3 (NIV)**

¹³ʻFor **Adam** was formed first, then **Eve**. ¹⁴And **Adam** was not the one deceived; it was the woman who was deceived and became a sinner'. **1 Timothy 2:13-14 (NIV)**

⁴⁵ʻ*So it is written: "The* **first man Adam** *became a living being"*⁽ᵃ⁾*; the last Adam, a life-giving spirit.* ⁴⁶*The spiritual did not come first, but the natural, and after that the spiritual.* ⁴⁷*The first* **man was of the dust of the earth**; *the second man is of heaven'.* **1 Corinthians 15:45-47 (NIV)**

The contexts and meanings in the Bible are very clear. With all the incredible detail the Bible offers from origins, history, law, religious processes, measurements of structures, redemption and prophecies concerning the future; there is no indication at all of any common ancestor with animals. We therefore have complete consistency throughout the whole of the Bible regarding Adam and Eve as historical figures and the first ancestors to have walked in the world, Adam having been made from the dust of the earth.

This naturally makes the whole philosophy of picking and choosing what you want to believe very difficult, as you would literally need to remove large portions of the Bible from every section of scripture to fit a particular world view or philosophical narrative. It is easy to simply live life and ignore the very principles our own society is even based on. The whole reason why we have a 7-day week, is due to Genesis 1, with God creating the universe and the world in 6 days and resting on the 7th. I thank God for the weekend! All doctrines in the Bible therefore go back to Genesis chapter 1 to 11.

If we decide not to adhere to a literalist interpretation of the Bible, then the whole aspect of religious practice becomes nonsense. If the account of the garden of Eden is a myth, then so is 'original sin'. The mythical story of the Fall would thus nullify the need for sacrifice, redemption, salvation and baptism. Ironically, the Catholic Church holds the Eucharist at the centre of their faith, although reject the idea of the Fall actually having happened as a realistic historical event. If this is the belief, then the ritualistic outworking of the faith would become completely futile.

We can't simply take 'On the Origin of Species' by Darwin to make it fit, or to try and keep both sides of the camp in the creation debate happy. A simple alteration to doctrine and proclamation of new philosophy regarding scripture based on the interpretation of a word, thereby throwing the rest of scripture out of divine balance raises some serious questions.

The word **'Yom'**, meaning **'day'**, or in some circumstance 'age', needs no different interpretation, especially in the context of the way it is communicated. If non-literalists want to link Darwinism with Genesis, thus throwing in expanses of 'ages' and time based on the word **'Yom'**, then some important considerations need to be made. The word 'Yom', is also used in the 10 commandments, in respect of the day of rest. I am sure we would love to have an 'age' off for the day of rest, but there is no getting around it; 24 hours is the context of the word. Placing very careful attention to the word 'day' (**Yom**), the writer of Genesis traditionally attributed to Moses receiving the word directly from God, throws up some very important repetitions. Please pay close attention to the bold font. The emphasis in Genesis Chapter 1: 1-31 is undeniable, as every day includes the statement *'So the evening and the morning were the ... day'*. This can only be a 24-hour period.

Upon closer inspection, it almost seems like God wrote in a pre-emptive strike to ensure the validity and historical accuracy and meaning could not be misinterpreted. It is quite evident that you need a lot of help to misunderstand what is written here. Genesis 1 thus forms a chronological account of the creation of the world and universe with God resting on the

7th day. Evening and morning are impossible to interpret in any other way than a 24-hour period.

To attempt to substantiate Genesis as a myth, one would have to suggest that Genesis 1 and 2 are separate creation stories. The whole theory, that Genesis 2 was written before Genesis 1 based on the evidence presented is also questionable. It is important to state, that Genesis 1 is in chronological order, whereas Genesis 2 is a historical narrative pertaining more to the 6th day in Genesis 1. It fills in the detail, and does not need to be in chronological order. This poses no problem for the full account of creation. The other important thing to consider, is that scripture originally written in Hebrew did not have chapters and verses added until later on, so nit picking the account based on later additions of numeric organization is also highly questionable. If the numeric chapters and verses were never there in the first place, but added later, the whole theory of two creation accounts falls apart. If we view historical accounts, specifically of nonfiction, it is usually not considered a problem if a chronological account is given with some narrative added later on for more detail and clarity.

People will always try and attack the origin beliefs of Orthodox Judaism or Evangelical Christianity by attempting to discredit the creation accounts. The main argument is usually regarding light, darkness and plant growth. Plants were created on the 3rd day, whereas the sun and moon were created on the 4th day. The answer to this is quite simple. If light was created on the first day and God is not just the creator, but the sustainer, then this does not become an issue. It is unlikely people will say there cannot be plant life in paradise (heaven), as there is no sun to be seen. The glory of God is likely to sustain and light up everything. If this is so difficult to believe, then the belief in heaven would also pose a challenge.

The word of God defends itself if it is read in detail and understood. One of the issues evangelicals will have with non-literalist interpretations is regarding the importance of the creation account. If Adam and Eve are not the first human beings, and creation took place according to accepted scientific accounts of the Big Bang and Evolution, where is the design and purpose of God in all this? The Big Bang is sold to us as one big accident, whereas evolution is depicted as undesigned and an unguided process of random mutations bringing forth variety of life in a massively long-time frame. If church teaching suggests we do not literally come from Adam, then it also needs to explain when the animal kingdom crossed over into humanity, especially in view of the dignity of the human person. There is still great emphasis of us being made in the image and likeness of God, yet nullified as a matter of fact. The other question in regard to this, is that there is no teaching even among non-literalists that suggest animals have a soul and partake in redemption. The Catholic Church still teaches we are made in the image and likeness of God, but then suggests it never happened. Equally, the Vatican believes that only humans have a soul. If humanity comes from the animal kingdom, then at what point did God decide for the soul to enter the body? As mentioned earlier, you need a lot of help to misunderstand what is written: furthermore, if it isn't broken, why are people trying to dilute it and fix it? The modern-day Church is trying to make the Bible correspond with theories that have only been proven to be fact by dogma and not by actual evidence in any field. This is why it is also important to view Darwin based on the evidence he actually had available and how we would interpret his evidence in the modern era.

Literalists will not just completely reject the evolutionary theory based on the origins of man, they will also reject George Lemaitre's theory of the Big Bang, as it is completely at odds with Genesis. The big bang idea comes out of explaining the world based on the laws of time and nature—basically, naturalism. As previously explained, the inventor of this theory **George Lemaître** a Jesuit priest kept his religious beliefs and what he called his science clearly separated, saying that his big bang idea left the materialist free to deny God's existence. Of course, the big bang is not operational science (i.e., testable, observable, or repeatable) but historical science (i.e., assumptions about the unobservable past). The big bang *is* really a religion that is used by most astronomers to explain away God. They theorize the universe is 13.7 billion years old.

Evangelicals will hold to a literalist view of the Bible for a variety of reasons, most of which I have mentioned above. The key issue with attempting to harmonize Biblical accounts with evolutionary theories poses a big problem, as the order of events are completely different than non-literalist would suggest. Scripture is clear that the creation process was finished and that it was very good – evolution teaches that the processes of change and adaption are creative processes that are still taking place. The whole account of original sin and man disobeying God is something we know as the Fall. This is when the whole of creation fell and became corrupted due to man's abuse of free will. Evolution teaches that struggle and death is good, furthermore necessary for the strong to survive.

The evolutionary theory is the exact antitheses of scripture and forms everything but an example for Bible believing Christians to follow. This is why Evangelicals hold the biblical standard. With all the incredible detail the Bible offers from origins, history, law, religious processes, measurements of structures, redemption and prophecies concerning the future, there is no indication at all of any common ancestor with animals. We therefore have complete consistency throughout the whole of the Bible regarding Adam and Eve as historical figures and the first ancestors to have walked in the world, Adam having been made from the dust of the earth. This naturally makes the whole philosophy of picking and choosing what you want to believe very difficult, as you would literally need to remove large portions of the Bible from every section of scripture to fit a particular world view or philosophical narrative.

Modern day science has eroded the concept of the Bible having any value in society, especially on the study of origins e.g. Christians should just leave the test tubes and the laboratories to the Atheists in white coats. The first chapter of this book, however, shows us that this could not be further from the truth. It is also fascinating to have a closer look into what the Bible has contributed to scientific understanding of the world. As mentioned before, all science consists of is a body of knowledge, not exclusively disregarding what is written in the world's best seller. Ironically the Bible is the most sold book in the world, unfortunately the least read and probably even less well understood, especially by many who claim to be wise.

The Bible: A written record of discovery

There was a time in our history when people thought the earth was piggy backed on an animal, or up until fairly recent history, the Church was convinced the earth was flat. Admittedly, there has been an upsurge in this belief as of late, but the Bible was fast to comment on the form of the earth, even before the famous mathematicians like Pythagoras, or the geographer Eratosthenes, philosopher Aristotle or theologian and astronomer Galileo. Had they taken **Isaiah 40:22** into account, it may have answered a lot of questions.

The laws of Thermodynamics are firmly set in the Bible. The first of which comes into play in Genesis 2:1. This law affirms that neither matter or energy can be either created or destroyed. There is no creating going on (ex nihilo), neither can anything be fully destroyed. This verse makes it evidently clear that it was all done i.e. finished, never to be re-started or undone. The second law of Thermodynamics teaches us that in all physical processes, everything becomes a little less ordered and structured. It is all slowly fading out through wear and tear as energy becomes less potent. This process teaches us that the universe in itself is not eternal and will eventually give of its last. This process is explained to us in Psalm 102: 25-26.

Looking at the very origins of human life which this book is mainly about, it is difficult to ignore what the Bible tells us in Genesis, that Adam was formed from the dust of the earth, and that God breathed into Adam's nostrils and he became a living soul. Darwin taught that Humanity was formed from primordial soup. Could it be that Darwin needs to be re-interpreted? Sir Fred Hoyle, professor of astronomy made the following statement concerning modern thought:

'No matter how large the environment one considers, life cannot have had a random beginning. Troops of monkeys thundering away at random on typewriters could not produce the works of Shakespeare, for the practical reason that the whole observable universe is not large enough to contain the necessary monkey hordes, the necessary typewriters, and certainly not the waste paper baskets required for the deposition of wrong attempts. The same is true for living material.... The likelihood of the spontaneous formation of life from inanimate matter is one to a number with 40,000 noughts after it.... It is big enough to bury Darwin and the whole theory of evolution. There was no primeval soup, neither on this planet nor on any other, and if the beginnings of life were not random, they must therefore have been the product of purposeful intelligence'. **Sir Fred Hoyle, professor of astronomy, Cambridge University**

(**Hoyle, F.** and C. Wickremasinghe. 1984. *Evolution from Space*. New York: Simon & Schuster, p 148.)

Can one really deny the contribution to science Genesis has made concerning the origins of man? The rejection of Darwin's theory of the origins of man is not reserved for creationists alone. The clarity of the sexes is also very prevalent in the Bible. Male and Female in Genesis and in Matthew 19:4 gives us an insight into the origin and importance of gender. This may be ignored as something completely irrelevant, but these early writings show us that life cannot continue without male and female. The one sex is completely dependent on the other. This is why God created a helper for Adam, not just for company, but also for procreation. One of the commandments in Genesis was to be fruitful and multiply. All mammals, fish and birds require male and female and this is made clear in the first chapters of the Bible. This poses a problem for evolution, as life is supposed to have originated from a single sex organism, brought to life by a lightning strike as Darwin's warm little pond would have us believe. This gives no answers in regard to complex and complementary reproductive systems. How could life have originated and developed without reproductive systems that complement one another? The Bible has the answers to this, but science is unsatisfied and is attempting to work backwards and find evidence to the contrary. A matter of fact, some scientists are currently trying to push a paradigm, that there is indeed no male or female, ie: 'you are what you feel you are'.

We find in scripture Leviticus 17:11 that blood is the very source of life. There was a very strange practice as recently as a couple of hundred years ago whereby people who were ill were deliberately bled, as the theory suggested that the disease could be released from the body that way. Needless to say, we know now that blood is the very source of life. Many people lost their lives through this medical procedure, whereby science thought they had got it right. The Bible had already made this clear thousands of years before.

The Torah holds countless verses which are scientific marvels, showing the Hebrews how to stay healthy, not just in food laws, but hygiene ones as well. When dealing with disease, it is clear to us today that hands must always be washed under water which is moving, to remove the source of disease in order not to give it a breeding ground. Washing should therefore always take place under running water for the purpose of cleanliness, especially in view of keeping infections at bay in a medical facility. As recently as the 19th century, doctors were still washing their hands in basins of water. This was thought to be a clean environment; however, invisible germs lead to an untold amount of deaths. In 1845 Doctor Ignaz Semmelweis was shocked by the death rate of women giving birth in hospitals in Vienna. A 30% death rate of women following giving birth was a shocking statistic. Doctor Semmelweis's observation to solving this problem was key, as he took note of doctors handling or examining dead bodies, and then moving on to the ward with pregnant women. This was a time when invisible microscopic diseases were not in the medical books. He then formulated a plan and enforced the rule that Doctors should wash their hands before and after examinations in running water and the results were astounding. The death rate dropped from 30% to just 2%. This principle was well known and recorded in the book of Leviticus thousands of years ago. Leviticus 15:13 (Encyclopaedia Britannica)

The Torah also had it sorted in respect of caring for the sick and dividing the healthy from the sick in the form of quarantining. It took a long time for the field of medicine to discover how crucial separating people with infectious diseases was. The need for it was clear in scripture, furthermore was well understood. Historically we only see the practice of quarantining coming to the forefront as recently as the 17th century. 'It has been calculated that one-fourth to one-third of the total population of Europe, or 25 million persons, died from plague during the Black Death'. (Encyclopaedia Britannica) The situation was of course this bad, because the dead and the sick shared the same rooms as the rest of the family. At the time the spread of the disease was blamed on 'bad air', or sometimes the demonic. Had they used the knowledge of the book of Leviticus, the situation could have been brought under control much quicker.

[46]'All the days wherein the plague shall be in him he shall be defiled; he is unclean: he shall dwell alone; without the camp shall his habitation be'. **Leviticus 13:46 (KJV)**

Scientifically there is also much to be said for the benefit of Kosher eating. Jewish food eating laws have always been seen as being a bit extreme, but on closer inspection we would need to see what is banned under the food eating laws. The book of Leviticus was clear concerning what the people were allowed to eat in the hot climate and what was actually banned. It is not difficult to work out why God banned these foods for the Hebrews when the law was given in the desert. Verses 1-23, gave the full list of what was permissible to eat and what was not. You may be wondering what the point of all that was, but scientifically we now know the health implications of eating these creatures, especially in a hot climate. All creatures mentioned on the food ban are high in parasites. To set the record straight, to kill all the parasites in pork, you need to grill the chop to the size of a biscuit to deal with all the microbes in the meat properly. Furthermore, we now know that all shell fish or fish without scales or fins are likely to be ocean bottom cleaners, will scavenge and eat excrement to purify the water. All high in unhelpful microbes.

Examples of food permissible to be eaten according to Kosher food eating instructions are listed below, as they do not fall under the forbidden list:

- Livestock - cow, deer, lamb, buffalo, elk, goat, moose
- Fish - bass, bluefish, crappie, perch, pike, salmon, sunfish, trout
- Birds - chicken, pheasant, grouse, quail
- Insects - locusts, crickets, grasshoppers

To add to this, there are specific parts of the body of these animals that are also not allowed to be consumed. Certain non-kosher animal parts, like the tail, the sciatic nerve and some fats generally found in the hindquarters, are separated for obvious reasons. Experts say the benefit also of kosher eating is because all kosher meats are thoroughly salted, therefore, may be less likely to carry E. coli and salmonella. The separation of meat and dairy also safeguards against cross contamination. God knew these foods were not advised for the Hebrews in the climate they were living in, something we scientifically have only got to grasp with in recent history. I am not suggesting we all eat Kosher, but I am making the point that healthy diet was recorded for a reason we are only able to now scientifically understand, especially during a time when there is much concern regarding processed foods, contaminants, genetically modified produce and an upsurge of allergies. The Corona virus has been traditionally attributed to the eating of bats and rats, all outlawed by the book of Leviticus.

Studying Leviticus, it can be seen that reptiles were off the menu, speaking of which, it was only till fairly recent history that it was discovered that snakes used to have legs (National Geographic 2016). The book of Genesis confirms that serpents used to have legs already in the 3rd chapter.

> *¹⁴ So the* LORD *God said to the **serpent:** "Because you have done this,*
> *You are cursed more than all cattle, And more than every beast of the field;*
> **On your belly you shall go, And you shall eat dust All the days of your life.**
> *¹⁵ And I will put enmity, Between you and the woman, And between your seed and her Seed;*
> *He shall bruise your head, And you shall bruise His heel'.*
> **Genesis 3:14-15 (NKJV)**

To a large extent science had been ignorant of the existence of invisible elements such as atoms, until more sophisticated technology had been developed to study atoms and particles. The Bible already pointed out these elements in Hebrews:

> *³ Through faith we understand that the worlds were framed by the word of God, so that things which are seen were not made of things which do appear'.* **Hebrews 11:3**

Atheistic science has desired to downgrade the Bible as legends and myths, but considering the vast amount of wisdom identified on a scientific level, these claims are largely down to ignorance of existing historical records of old, rather than well researched evidence of historical science. It is true these evidences are not recent and how could they be? But many of the points made above do confirm, that what was considered to be evidence-based science many a time, failed to recognise what was already established firmly in the word of God. Augustine defined science as: 'anything to do with knowledge of the temporal world'. Thomas Aquinas considered theology a science because it encounters 'special and general revelation'.

Darwin: Science or Science Fiction?

How would we have viewed Darwin's book if it had been written today? Would we have viewed it as science or science fiction? I think with all our advances in science there would have been many questions in regard to the first replicating cell. Darwin's time marked a period of literary success; one book which especially comes to mind is taught in many schools for the purpose of English exams. Frankenstein is a novel written by British author Mary Shelly about the eccentric scientist Victor Frankenstein, who creates a creature in an unorthodox scientific experiment. This novel was published in 1818. This is just another example of matter colliding with energy leading to consciousness. It is a novel which comes under the fiction category of the library. Man, even with all scientific advances today has been unable to bring anything to life or consciousness on purpose, let alone by random chance, even if the biological matter was available. It is this mystical force of electricity in the 19th century that sparked the imagination. This era marked some ground-breaking discoveries in the field of science. It was this time when science was being birthed as a belief system and the discovery of electricity left no boundaries for future possibilities.

This was the century in which Charles Darwin sailed on the Beagle in 1831 and in 1835, made interesting discoveries concerning micro evolution with turtles and finches in the Galapagos Islands. The locals were able to tell which tortoise came from certain islands and that each island was perceived to have different species of finches. He concluded that all the finches on the islands needed to have originated from an original couple of finches. After his many observations and further conclusions of the survival of the fittest, his first work 'On the Origin of Species', was published in 1859. There has never been a published scientific work that has shaped the world into a streamlined view, permeating the way we perceive the physical, biological and psychological sciences. Darwin's book has not just been confined to these fields, but has affected decisions made in history and more recently Christian Theology as well, in particular forming part of the teachings of the Catholic Church. It was through Darwin's book that we saw an alternative belief system develop that challenged the account given to us in scripture. He didn't specifically give an explanation regarding the origin of life itself, which one would have thought he would have done given the title of his book, but he did theorize a theory in a letter to a friend. Microscopes were not particularly well understood in those days; however, it did not seem unreasonable to assume that life itself could have emerged by a chance combination of a variety of chemicals.

'But if we could conceive in some warm little pond, with all sorts of ammonia and phosphoric salts, light, heat, electricity.... present, that a protein compound was chemically formed ready to undergo still more complex changes'. (Letter sometimes dated 1871, Darwin to Charles Hooker dated March 29, 1863)

He was cautious in his approach to the subject of the origin of all life: however, spontaneous chemical generation was indeed the theory he was leaning towards. It was Thomas Huxley who enthusiastically developed the theory relating to primordial slime, then before long by the development of others, the biology text books we all had in school reflected the idea of the primordial soup and Darwin's warm little pond. This was not presented as theory, but as fact. The twentieth century's rendition of Darwin's warm little pond can be visually imagined by energy colliding with the primordial soup to produce the first living cell.

The question however is, can matter and energy create organic life? The 1953 'origins of life experiment', by Stanley

Miller allegedly at first did just that. He managed to produce primitive amino acids, by recreating what he envisaged to be the primordial soup consisting of methane, ammonia, hydrogen and water vapour. Primitive amino acids, however, were a far cry from the first living cell and in the 1960s this theory was reviewed by geo-chemists as they realised that hydrogen would have escaped this whole process. The experiment was repeated by Stanley Miller this time with just carbon dioxide, nitrogen and water vapour. The results were disappointing for him, as the results concluded with no development of primitive amino acids. Even if it were possible under these conditions, the question as a direct consequence has to be asked, whether primitive acids dissolved in the ocean can give you a living cell? Biologist Jonathan Wells from the Discovery Institute of the University of California does not seem to think so. His reasoning is as follows:

'If you create a perfect environment for a living cell in a test-tube to survive and place a living cell inside, then take a sterile needle and puncture it, all the molecules leak out of the cell. After this, you will not be able to make a living cell out of these molecules. You cannot put Humpty Dumpty together again. You are still millions of miles from creating a living cell. There is no theory that has finalised how basic chemical components could have arranged themselves into the first living cell'.
(Jonathan Wells, Illustra Media)

Even Stanley Miller who initially through his origins of life experiment converted many to Atheism admitted in 1991:

'The origins of life has turned out to be much more difficult than I, and most other people, envisioned'.
(Horgan, 'In the Beginning', Scientific American, Vol 264 p 100-109, 2 Feb 1991)

What do Evolutionists say?

If there has ever been a scientist in recent history excited about evolution, it would have to be Richard Dawkins. He has indeed been the cover-boy of the century in regard to evolution, almost in an evangelistic way. His admissions however, seem to verify the same dilemma:

'The theory we seek, of the origin of life on this planet, should therefore positively not be a plausible theory'!
(Richard Dawkins (Ph.D, Professor of Zoology), The Greatest Show on Earth: The Evidence for Evolution, 2009, p. 422.)

The 2008 interview with Ben Stein was, however, more intriguing. Dawkins confirmed that he views people who even believe in Intelligent Design as relatively lacking in common sense or not worthy of being taken seriously. He made a number of shocking admissions. He repeated the same admission twice, that *no one knows how life originally started*, although speaking of the origin of the first self-replicating molecule. This is simply not Darwinian and a highly unlikely response you would expect from a person everyone has championed as a hero for atheistic evolution. To add another truth bomb, he then suggests that life could have originated due to some sort of signature of a designer from a civilisation somewhere out in the universe, not to forget of course *'by some kind of Darwinian means'*. This is when speculation and science fiction combined becomes a plausible theory based on who is speculating. The interviewer, Ben Stein, was quick to point out that Dawkins had effectively snookered himself by admitting clear references to intelligent design and a designer. This is the teleological theory presented in perfection. If it is designed, then there is a designer and the designer must be God!

If we carefully look at the admissions of some scientists, it is clear that the same questions still exist today as they did whilst Darwin was still alive. It is also evident that it is unlikely any scientists actually believe in evolution the way Darwin had first envisaged. So, what we have instead is a form of Neo-Darwinism that only identifies with certain points of Darwinian evolution. It is ironic that in over 150 years, reality tells us that no progress in any field of scientific endeavour has managed to supply us with any explanation whatsoever concerning the origins of life. Scientists will spend many years qualifying in a particular field of micro study and then impose a particular 'world view' on that micro study. Doctor John Lennox from Oxford University makes the interesting point, that instead of science forming a 'world view', the opposite takes place, in that biases in our own 'world view', effectively dictate our science (Stein 2007). To add to this micro study of the world we then have this narrow sliver of discovery taking on a philosophical form. Einstein was quick to point out the dangers of this approach:

'The man of science is a poor philosopher'. **Albert Einstein** (Albert Einstein (2016). "The Albert Einstein Collection: Essays in Humanism, The Theory of Relativity, and "The World As I See It", p.116, Open Road Media)

The Numbers Lottery

It is important to remember that within Darwinian evolution, the origins and development of life theory relies ultimately on an undirected process, completely devoid of any design, purpose or plan, thus making it incompatible with a creator. The Teleological theory clearly sets out rules and parameters for design and purpose.

Design will always take into account the laws of mathematics (biological coding), especially when we look at the subject of DNA. We have just discussed self-replicating molecules in the form of the first living cell, although yet to be proven beyond a shadow of a doubt. DNA is a very long chain of molecules that also requires digital information for the function of the cell. It is coded in four letters almost forming an infinitely long sentence. The segments of DNA appear in two strands that need to complement each other in order to replicate. To summarize, if they do not complement each other with perhaps 3 billion pieces of information needing to appear in an exact order, then no replication takes place. This of course does not allow for mistakes. Macro evolution takes things even a step further. It requires mutations bringing about new pieces of information to bring about a change. The theory of evolution relies completely on this concept. This would be a change in DNA, which is effectively the hereditary material of life. DNA affects everything from behaviour, to its appearance and physiology. It is the change in an organism's DNA that alters all aspects of its life, which is called a mutation. Darwinism therefore relies completely on small successive mutations altering structures to new forms and species. In other words, without mutation evolution cannot take place. These are considered to change from generation to generation. So what did Darwin effectively say about his own theory in regard to small changes taking place in 'On the Origin of Species'?

> *'If it could be demonstrated that any complex organ existed, which could not possibly have been formed by numerous, successive slight modifications my theory would absolutely break down'.*
> (Darwin, 'On the Origin of Species', 1859)

It is evident that Darwin's theory revolves completely around the absence of any type of design of biological machinery or coding sequences of DNA. Aspects of design cannot be explained away by naturalistic means. In many respects one may actually wonder if he managed to negate his own theory by this one sentence. It is however evidentially true that it is mainly his successors who popularized the idea of small successive mutations being possible in macro evolution. The small successive changes within species in the form of micro evolution no one argues with as the genetic information allows it. I do not know any Christian who does not believe in micro evolution. One only needs to take the example of the bull finches' beaks, or wolves being domesticated to see micro evolution in process. However, they are clearly defined as within their own species, not species turning into separate species or kinds (macro evolution).

Micro evolution is explained easiest within dogs. Micro evolution is evident in all form of dogs, but it is clear that it is the wolf (common ancestor) at the top of the DNA chain that possesses all the genetic information necessary to breed down to a Chihuahua. There is no miracle possible to use the lack of DNA information in the Chihuahua to breed back up to the wolf, as large portions of the DNA information have now been lost. This is also the precise problem with the theory of macro evolution being a possibility. In natural selection it is only possible to take from the genetic information which is already available, not from new genetic information that is clearly not there. This is why it is not possible to observe one specie turning into another. Neither is it evident in the fossil record.

Biology text books today include the existence of something called the tree of life illustrating a common ancestor. It may even include a chart of an upward progression of species in the form of a geologic time scale. Darwin's book 'On the

Origin of the Species', only alludes to a single illustration of this idea. The tree map does not represent the bio-diverse intensity illustrated in the theories we attribute to Darwin. Furthermore, with all the progress of analysis we have available to us now, we still cannot conclusively put our finger on the clear evidence to the origin of all life. Evolution requires small successive mutations to be validated, yet the evidence available to us is to the contrary. It requires the idea of endless new genetic information appearing from nowhere, from the first replicating cell to the development of the sexes and the immense biodiversity we have today in all shapes and sizes. Here are some reminders concerning this issue:

'The typical mutation is very mild. It usually has no effect, but shows up as a small decrease in viability or fertility. Each mutation leads ultimately to one genetic death'.

(James Crow, Professor of Genetics, University of Wisconsin, 1997)

"DNA is an information code. The overwhelming conclusion is that information does not and cannot arise spontaneously by mechanistic processes. Intelligence is a necessity in the origin of any informational code, including the genetic code, no matter how much time is given."

(Lane Lester (Ph.D, Genetics) and Ray Bohlin (Ph.D. Molecular and Cell Biology), The Natural Limits to Biological Change, 1989, p 157.)

"But in all the reading I've done in the life-sciences literature, I've never found a mutation that added information."

(Lee Spetner (Ph.D. Physics), John Hopkins University, Not By Chance, 1997, pp. 131,138)

"It seems fair to point out that evolutionists have yet to provide even a single concrete example of a mutation leading to an increase of information as requested." (Royal Truman (Ph.D. Chemistry) The Problem of Information for the Theory of Evolution', 2002, p. 14.)

'About 4 in 10,000 of known mutations are presumed to be beneficial. However, these are only beneficial in a very narrow sense since they involve a loss of function. Not one of these mutations unambiguously created new information'.

(Jerry Bergman, Ph.D. Human Biology, Research on the Deterioration of the genome and Darwinism: Why mutations result in the degeneration of the genome, 2004)

To put things simply, the rules of probability come into play massively. These probabilities are calculated in the likelihood of related mutations. 2 related mutations are put in the realm of 1 in 100 trillion. 3 related mutations are estimated as one in a billion trillion. You can only imagine what the probability of 4 related mutations might be. It is also important to know the difference between mutations and simply new traits emerging based on the genetic information that was already available when genes switch on and off. This is characterized in different patterns of an animal's fur, or cats not having a tail, furthermore different eye colour. The small successive mutations Darwin was likely to have been pointing towards were higher levels of functioning. As we have discovered, there is no evidence available pointing toward an upward evolutionary process, rather observations of genetic death. The genome was not something Darwin had envisaged, especially the realms of impossibility to randomly produce one.

The Ancestors recorded in Bible History

In the study of origins, 'ancestor' is of course the word that most of us cling to with great interest. We want to know about our unobservable past; we want to also know where we come from. This is what generates the interest in ancestry websites and the need to know who our fore-fathers were, what they did and how they behaved. This is when the old family photo albums become interesting and the stories that are told by family who are still alive. It is this cornerstone that gives us meaning and the possible longing for a privileged past. It is within these foundations that we define ourselves, or on the contrary choose to make a change for the better. Ancestry is however a limiting factor, in that one eventually stumbles upon the end of the record, that picture or document that wasn't passed down, that name change or incomplete record at the registry office. In the case of the Bible however, the genealogy records are complete, all the way from Jesus back to Adam in Luke chapter 3. The Jews were meticulous record keepers. Scribes would not just copy, they did things in a mathematical process, counting even letters on lines triple checked by other scribes. To the Bible believing Christian, there is of course no missing link. The picture is complete and does not form a gap filling exercise to fill in the blanks. The discovery of truth is therefore manifest not in just reading God's word, but also studying it.

For others, belief in the origins of man being created in the image and likeness of God on a literal basis can only progress by viewing life through a laboratory test tube. This is where the study of Y-Chromosomal Adam and Mitochondrial Eve enters the stage. "Y-Chromosomal Adam" and "Mitochondrial Eve" are the scientifically-proven theories that every man alive today is descended from a single man and every man and woman alive today is descended from a single woman. They concluded that humanity must have experienced a genetic bottleneck in the past, which may not have been as infinitely far back as many would like to suggest. Further to their study, it was found that every man alive today actually descended from a single man whom scientists now refer to as "Y-Chromosomal Adam." Mitochondrial Eve is believed to be the mother of all living humans, male and female. (Dorit, R.L., Akashi, H. and Gilbert, W. "Absence of polymorphism at the ZFY locus on the human Y chromosome." 1995)

It is difficult for evolutionists to deny this. However, there will be discrepancies in regard to whether these original humans lived at the same time according to different scientific studies. These would however likely be assumptions rather than fact. The time-frame within the parameters of Darwinian thought is of course very different from the Biblical view. One truth we can derive from the study is; that every man today is descendant from one man, and every human alive is descended from one woman. This also corresponds with scripture:

'And Adam called his wife's name Eve; because she was the mother of all living'. (Genesis 3:20) **NKJ**

The allusive Primordial Ancestor

There have been many attempts in evolution to prove the natural selection theory as fact. The perfect evidence would be to discover a humanoid that could at least be seen as transitioning to humans we have today. History throws up a number of interesting discoveries that caused a massive ripple of excitement in their time: however, have lost their appeal as further evidence has exposed them as outright frauds. This is the very problem evolution has to deal with i.e. it is in constant need of re-inventing itself or at the very least forensically working its way back to finalize the evidence to prove a theory to be true beyond a shadow of a doubt. This doubt you evidentially will not see in the text books. You will just have proclaimed evidence until debunked.

Here are a number of examples that may still be used as evidence today, although they have been thoroughly discredited from time. Lucy, Heidelberg man, Nebraska man, Piltdown man, Peking man, Neanderthal man, New Guinea man and Cro-Magnon man have been thoroughly discredited over the years, yet some still appear in the text books.

With all the evidences that are presented as missing links, it may be worth looking at the Guinness book of records to discover what record-breaking humans we still have alive today, which do indeed fit descriptions of supposed missing links, varying in height, weight and skull formation. Actually, travelling further afield will confirm the existence of perfectly normal people considered by some to be extraordinary.

The ancestral worship still persists. A verified missing link announced as the final proof of evolution has not emerged in a strong serious capacity for quite a while. Probably due to the fascination of the study of aliens and the possibility of seeding of humanity from another planet, as discussed in one of the previous chapters. Nevertheless, Sir David Attenborough made a fascinating claim in 2009, which was reported in the UK on every news channel and in most papers. This was a coordinated effort even by Google, as it changed its logo on the same day of the announcement to promote the evolutionary discovery of Ida.

'Fossil Ida, extraordinary find is 'missing link', in human evolution', was the hypothesis. *'The evidence was now complete and it would have met the approval of Darwin'*, Sir

David claimed. (*The Guardian Tuesday 19th May 2009)* The talk of the finding of 'Ida', however, disappeared as quickly as it came. The massive news coverage and the trigger words 'approval from Darwin', caused as they always do an enormous amount of interest. When the peer reviews were released, it came as no surprise that the fossil seemed to have little difference to ordinary lemurs or lorises. In every sense, it was basically an admission that the link always has been missing, furthermore goes down in history as yet another failed attempt at providing credible evidence. The holy grail of fossils quickly turned into a holy fail of paleontology.

One might question why DNA has been insufficient to deter further research in something that has no more than emotional significance relating to the desire of confirming a pet theory. Y-Chromosomal Adam and Mitochondrial Eve provide us with the answers we need, but not necessarily the origins most scientists want. Science itself is plagued by the inclusion and rejection of evidence based on a person's pet theory, which we can more or likely agree, usually leans toward attempting to prove evolution in a never-ending paradigm of hype, disappointment and cover up.

The Social Impact of Darwinian thought

What impact has Darwinism had on society? We can only turn to history to give us this answer. Social Darwinism has indeed had a very strong influence on the way people have developed the idea of a human community. If we toy with the ideas of natural evolution and with the notion that species have not been created but came about by random chance, then for the sake of putting humanity in any kind of moralistic framework, then some kind of ethical structure needs to be derived from the process. Darwinism, therefore, has not just completely changed the way we view science and the world, forming a world view on just science, but rather on the way we view society as a whole. As discussed earlier, Darwinism has framed an approach to viewing life through the lens of a scientific test tube, creating a worldview about the existence of society and not just the forming of a simple scientific hypothesis. Darwinian evolution has influenced our entire Western way of living, whereas, the theory has taken the place of the more traditional ways we understand life. In the past this led to massive social and political phenomena in the build up to the second world war. In the 1920s people were looking for solutions to problems in western society, ranging from crime to poverty or even sexual behaviour. They felt at the time that Darwinism could provide some explanations and solutions to these problems.

The dangers of these stances on complicated issues resulted in politics and culture being dehumanized, with a complete absence of the sanctity of life. This degrading process reduced humans to no more than biological machines or even animals. The justice system began to suffer the consequences of the lack of existence of 'free will', allowing any punishments to be shelved in favour of lobotomy. Departments of welfare suggested eradicating the economically disadvantaged by sterilization, especially those who were considered as biologically unfit, i.e. viewing people exclusively in economic terms. Business was permeated by racist ideas of human evolution, using advertising methods to influence consumer behaviour. Sexual behaviour was underpinned with a new form of morality, based on animal instincts rather than traditional morality based on the Bible or ethical teachings of the church. These ideas were developed in the West by biologists and anthropologists in the 1920s.

If we look at Europe, the Nazis themselves were fanatical Darwinists. Aside from the Holocaust itself, 15,000 handicapped people were killed as illness or deformity whether in the body or mind did not fit in with Nazi ethics or utopia. It is estimated that at least 200,000 individuals were murdered at euthanasia centres, with no holds barred at a person's age. Many of the victims were children carted off to death facilities. These actions were in keeping with the eugenics ideas about racial purity developed by German ideologies. While officially ended in 1941, the programme lasted until the German surrender in 1945. Nearly 15,000 German citizens were transported to the hospital and died there, most killed in a gas chamber. In addition, hundreds of forced labourers from Poland and other countries occupied by the Nazis were killed there.

Any government moving away from Judeo/Christian principles or adopting the ethics of Darwinism as the only foundation to explain life, is riddled with the worst human rights abuses known to man. If we look at all Atheistic states, we have the same pattern of devaluing of human life. Stalinist Russia saw 20 million deaths, merely as a result of Stalin's paranoia and need for absolute control. Mau's revolutionist China it is believed caused over 40 million deaths, supposedly for the greater good of humanity and equality. Cambodia suffered the annihilation of a third of the entire population. People were put to death for merely showing possible signs of being able to think for themselves and not part of a communist collective. The Holy book becomes the political manifesto of the country and the image to worship is the statue of the dictator.

The English philosopher Thomas Malthus, devoted a lot of his time studying population growth and the impact on the economy, especially the tendency of the poor to reproduce more rapidly than other classes in society. Malthus will always be linked to movements relating to population control.

'The ideas of Malthus were a significant influence on the inception of Darwin's theory of evolution.' (Charles Darwin:

gentleman naturalist, A biographical sketch by John van Wyhe, 2006)

Darwin was convinced by the notion that population growth would eventually lead to more organisms than could possibly survive in any given environment, leading him to theorize that organisms with a relative advantage in the struggle for survival and reproduction would be able to pass their characteristics on to further generations. Proponents of Malthusianism were in turn influenced by Darwin's ideas. These schools of thought influenced the field of eugenics. "humane birth selection through humane birth control" in order to avoid a Malthusian catastrophe by eliminating the "unfit". (Pierre Desrochers; Christine Hoffbauer (2009). "The Post War Intellectual Roots of the Population Bomb")

The full title of Darwin's book made his position very clear. 'On the Origin of Species, By Means of Natural Selection, on the Preservation of favoured Races in the struggle for life'. The 1859 title has since been modernised with certain words omitted to avoid unnecessary upset.

Eugenics is the practice or advocacy of improving the human species by selectively mating people with specific desirable hereditary traits. It aims to reduce human suffering by "breeding out" disease, disabilities and so-called undesirable characteristics from the human population. (Encyclopedia Britannica) The word "eugenics" was first used in 1883 by the English scientist Francis Galton, who was related to Charles Darwin. The idea was to promote the utopia of perfecting the human race in a process of exterminating "undesirables" and making sure that those coined "desirables" were multiplied. This is effectively social Darwinism as we know it, by breeding the fit, whilst giving nature a helping hand and getting rid of the unfit. The exact science of genetics was not fully understood in Darwin's day. However, the theory of evolution taught that species did change as a result of natural selection and that it would reap many benefits in cattle farming with selected, desirable strong breeds being multiplied. Eugenics in its outset is linked to planned parenthood in the Darwinian struggle for existence. Abortion, Infanticide and Euthanasia is a concept that seeks to rid society immediately of anyone who may be a drain on resources, thinking of people only in economic terms.

Effectively, the extermination of individuals can be considered as beneficial in the modern day as organs and other biological matter can be a booming business. Applying Darwinism to humanity boils down to a devaluing of human life, as the idea of transitioning life forms rids us of the idea of human privilege. The idea of only allowing the strong to breed is evident in Darwin's book 'Descent of Man'.

Concluding Remarks

We have undergone a long journey in the discussion of Philosophy and Science. We have discovered that belief in Neo-Darwinism when studying the facts carefully can only be compared with the story of 'The Emperor's New Clothes'. There is no actual scientific evidence of it being true, yet many choose to believe it due to the fear of being caught out or ridiculed. Furthermore, if you repeat something often enough, you eventually believe it to be so. We are living in a world that is increasingly moving away from the ethics of God's word, especially due to education and the media. Unfortunately, this is seen by many as progress. If we choose to deny the relevance or the inerrancy of scripture, the further we are likely to distance ourselves from God's truth. Furthermore, interpreting God's truth the way we want to perceive it becomes counterproductive.

According to church statistics, most young people never return to church after conducting further education. The main reason for this, is because they have been taught that the Bible is not true and merely a moralistic guide with some nice stories. In view of the future, this is a catastrophe for the Body of Christ as a whole.

We spend a great deal of time attempting to set the record straight in regard to the sanctity of life, abortion, euthanasia, racism, what constitutes a marriage, roles of men and women and sexual behaviour. However, we negate everything by downgrading scripture as myth and legend. Ironically many will readily want to believe what allegedly happened 20 million years ago, but will have trouble acknowledging what happened 2,000 years ago, although scribes wrote it down in the Bible as eye witnesses. If our world view incorporates the Bible as infallible, then one is more likely to live according to its statutes, especially in view of the dignity of the human person. This is why the study of the origins of man is so important, because we are truly made in God's image and likeness. It is really not difficult to work out, that the belief of a literal Adam and Eve and the fall of man is the only way we can put the whole of the Christian faith into its proper context. This incorporates our own personal need for forgiveness, redemption and love for our fellow man.

Creation: On the Origin of Man

BIBLIOGRAPHY

Augustine. *The Literal Meaning of Genesis, translated by John Hammond Taylor, Vol. 1, Book 4, Chapter 33, paragraph 51-52, p. 141, italics in the original. New York: Newman Press. (1982)*

Behe, M, J. *Darwin's Black Box: The Biochemical Challenge to Evolution, New York, The Free Press, (1996)*

Behe, M, J. *The Edge of Evolution: The Search for the limits of Darwinism, New York: Free Press, (2008)*

Bergman Jerry, *Ph.D. Human Biology, Research on the Deterioration of the Genome and Darwinism: Why mutations result in the degeneration of the genome, (2004)*

Boyd, Steven W. *The Biblical Hebrew Creation Account, Calvary University, (2018)*

Catechism of the Catholic Church

Crow James, *Professor of Genetics, University of Wisconsin, (1997)*

Darwin Charles, *The Descent of Man, and Selection in Relation to Sex, (1871)*

Darwin Charles, *On the Origin of Species, By Means of Natural Selection, on the Preservation of favoured Races in the Struggle for life, (1859)*

Dawkins Richard *(Ph.D, Professor of Zoology), The Greatest Show on Earth: The Evidence for Evolution, p. 422. (2009)*

Dei Verbum 12

Desrochers Pierre; *Christine Hoffbauer "The Post War Intellectual Roots of the Population Bomb". (2009)*

Dorit, R.L., Akashi, H. and Gilbert, W. *"Absence of polymorphism at the ZFY locus on the human Y chromosome." Science 268:1183-1185, (1995)*

Einstein Albert *"The Albert Einstein Collection: Essays in Humanism, The Theory of Relativity, and The World as I See It", p.116, Open Road Media. (2016)*

Encyclopaedia Britannica

Gaudium et Spes

Holy Bible *NKJ*

Holy Bible *NIV*

Holden Constance, *"The Politics of Palaeoanthropology," Science, p.737, August 14, (1981)*

Holye, F. and C. Wickremasinghe. *Evolution from Space. New York: Simon & Schuster, 148. (1984)*

Horgan, *'In the Beginning', Scientific American, Vol 264 p 100-109, 2 Feb (1991)*

Kragh Helge, *Cosmology and Controversy: The Historical Development of Two Theories of the Universe, Princeton University Press, (1996)*

Lemaitre George, *'The Primeval Atom Hypothesis and the Problem of Clusters of Galaxies, in R Stoops, La Structure et l'Evolution de l'Universe, (1958) 1-32. As translated in Helge Kragh, Cosmology and Controversy; The Historical Development of Two Theories of the Universe (1996) 60)*

Lester Lane *(Ph.D, Genetics) and Ray Bohlin (Ph.D. Molecular and Cell Biology), The Natural Limits to Biological Change, p 157. (1989)*

National Geographic 2016

Patrizia Barbera: *Todgeweihte kamen in Postbussen zur Hinrichtung, in Frankfurter Allgemeine Zeitung, page 55, 21 October (2008)*

Spetner Lee *(Ph.D. Physics), John Hopkins University, Not by Chance, pp. 131,138, (1997)*

Stein Ben, *'Expelled, No Intelligence Allowed', Premise Media Corporation (2008)*

Strobel Lee, *The Case for a Creator, Illustra Media, (2006)*

The Guardian, *Fossil Ida: Extraordinary find is 'missing link' in human evolution, Tuesday 19th May (2009)*

The Guardian, *Piltdown Man, British Archaeologies' greatest Hoax, 4th Feb (2012)*

Tomkins Jeffrey *(Ph.d Genetics), Engineered Protein Evolution, Proves Biological Complexity', Acts and Facts, March (2013)*

Truman Royal *(Ph.D. Chemistry) The Problem of Information for the Theory of Evolution', p. 14 (2002)*

Tuttle Russell H., *Natural History, p 64 quoted in Bones of Contention, p 174 March (1990)*

Van Wyhe' John, *'Charles Darwin: gentleman naturalist', A biographical sketch, (2006)*

Weikart Richard, *From Darwin to Hitler, Evolutionary Ethics, Eugenics and Racism in Germany, Palgrave Macmillan US, (2004)*

West Dr John *'G.,Darwin Day in America: How Our Politics and Culture Have Been Dehumanized in the Name of Science (2007)*

Yockey Hubert, *(Ph.D. Physics), Information Theory, Evolution, and the Origin of life, p. 188 (2005)*

FIRST BOOK BY THIS AUTHOR

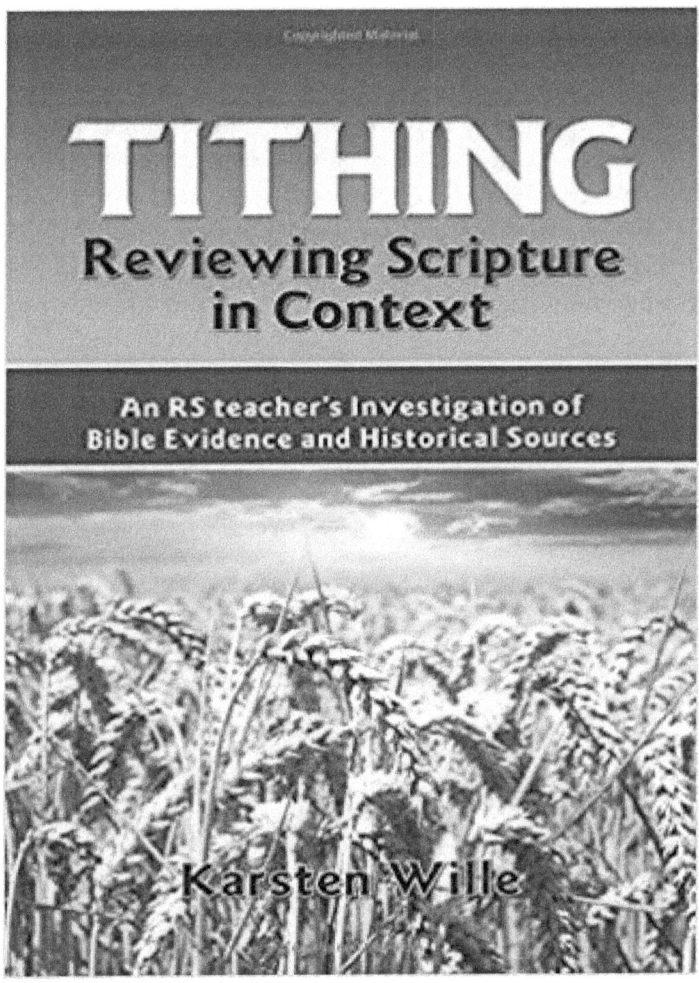

This book analyses tithing in the context of Biblical scripture. Tithing is mentioned many times in the Bible and many theories have been developed over time especially concerning the possible need of giving a tenth of one's income in the New

Testament Church. This subject has divided many people with a special focus on the Law as opposed to freewill giving. It is Karsten's intention to delve into scripture, commenting on the customs and cultures of the times they were written and the audiences they were meant to capture. Scripture is only useful if we rightly divide the word of truth, which is consequently only possible if we study ourselves approved (2 Timothy 2:15). Karsten summarizes all the main points of the study of scripture and context, then finalizes the findings in easy to navigate bullet points to form an overview, narrowing evidence into a systematic review. A clear picture of the subject arises, whereby you can determine your own conclusions regarding this topic.

ABOUT THE AUTHOR

Karsten is an award-winning author *'Tithing: Reviewing scripture in context'*. He has worked as a Pentecostal Pastor, planting churches in the UK and working in a Missions and Evangelism department ministering the Gospel in Africa, Asia and South America. With a PGCE from Exeter University and studies with the Open University in Educational Research, he has taught Religious Education in schools for 20 years with a keen interest in Apologetics.